YOU HAVE MORE
INFLUENCE
THAN YOU THINK

YOU HAVE MORE
INFLUENCE
THAN YOU THINK

How We Underestimate
Our Power of Persuasion,
and Why It Matters

Vanessa Bohns

W. W. NORTON & COMPANY
Independent Publishers Since 1923

For information about permission to reproduce selections from this book,
write to Permissions, W. W. Norton & Company, Inc.,
500 Fifth Avenue, New York, NY 10110

For information about special discounts for bulk purchases,
please contact W. W. Norton Special Sales at
specialsales@wwnorton.com or 800-233-4830

Manufacturing by Lake Book Manufacturing
Production manager: Devon Zahn

Library of Congress Cataloging-in-Publication Data

Names: Bohns, Vanessa K., author.
Title: You have more influence than you think : how we underestimate
our power of persuasion and why it matters / Vanessa Bohns.
Description: First edition. | New York, NY : W. W. Norton & Company, [2021]
| Includes bibliographical references and index.
Identifiers: LCCN 2021012207 | ISBN 9781324005711 (hardcover) |
ISBN 9781324005728 (epub)
Subjects: LCSH: Persuasion (Psychology) | Influence (Psychology)
Classification: LCC BF637.P4 B545 2021 | DDC 153.8/52—dc23
LC record available at https://lccn.loc.gov/2021012207

W. W. Norton & Company, Inc., 500 Fifth Avenue, New York, N.Y. 10110
www.wwnorton.com

W. W. Norton & Company Ltd., 15 Carlisle Street, London W1D 3BS

1 2 3 4 5 6 7 8 9 0

For Hanna and Evelyn

Contents

Introduction   ix

1   UNSEEN INFLUENCE   1

2   YOUR POWER OF PERSUASION   29

3   JUST BECAUSE YOU ASKED   53

4   WHY IT'S SO HARD TO SAY "NO"   75

5   MISINFORMATION, INAPPROPRIATE ASKS,
      AND ME TOO   99

6   POWER AND PERCEIVED INFLUENCE   125

7   SEEING, FEELING, AND EXPERIENCING
      YOUR INFLUENCE OVER OTHERS   157

Conclusion   191
Acknowledgments   195
Notes   199
Index   229

Introduction

I LOVE TEACHING, but from the lectern at the front of the room it can be hard to tell if you're having any impact at all. You pour your heart and soul into a lesson, only to stare out at a sea of unreadable faces, most of whom will disappear out the door the second class is over. Until one day, you get an email from a former student detailing the influence you had on their life, and, like a bolt of lightning, you experience a moment of teary-eyed recognition of the impact your words and actions can have on others.

Most of us, however, don't regularly get this sort of insight into how we influence others. Whether we affect others in big, life-changing ways (like EMTs or social workers) or in smaller, everyday ways (like good-humored baristas), we typically only gain insight into a very tiny sliver of our true impact. In other words, we may get one email for every hundred students we've taught. And because we rarely get insight into our influence over others, we may chronically underestimate it. After all, if hardly anyone tells you how good your compliment made them feel, or that they were smiling all day about that joke you told them, how would you know you had any impact at all?

Curious about this phenomenon, fellow psychologist Erica

Boothby and I thought up an experiment: What if we asked people before they engaged in an ordinary interaction with another person what they expected their impact on the other person to be, and then immediately asked the other person how much they were actually impacted? Would people underestimate the influence they have on others in these sorts of commonplace, everyday interactions?

We recruited people to participate in our study and told them that it essentially consisted of a single task: They were to leave the lab and go outside, approach a random stranger (of the same gender), and compliment them. We even told them what to compliment the stranger on: They were simply to say, "Hey, I like your shirt."

Before they left the lab, we asked our participants to guess how good this compliment would make the other person feel. Then we gave them an envelope to hand to the other person right after complimenting them. Inside the envelope was a survey asking the other person how good the compliment made them feel and a second envelope for the approached stranger to put their completed survey in and seal so our participants couldn't see what the other person had said (which could have made strangers less honest in their responses).

What we found in this study has changed the way I interact with strangers: If I have something nice to say to someone, I make the effort to say it. Because I now know my seemingly trivial, awkwardly phrased compliment will make the other person feel significantly happier than I think it will. The strangers participants approached and complimented in our study said they enjoyed the interaction and that the compliment made them feel more "flattered" and "good" than our participants expected it would when they imagined giving it. More than this, when we ran the study again and asked participants how annoyed and bothered people would feel being approached and complimented by a random stranger, participants thought their actions would be perceived as much more annoying and bothersome than the people who were approached reported actually feeling.[1,2]

And it's not simply about complimenting someone on their shirt. We found the same pattern of results when we asked participants to find something—anything—they genuinely liked about a random stranger to say to them. Overwhelmingly, the recipients of such praise appreciated it more than the people offering it anticipated.

So, people underestimate how good a simple compliment will make others feel, and overestimate how annoying it is to be stopped by a random stranger who wants to express their admiration. This phenomenon also goes beyond superficial praise. People also underestimate how appreciative and good it makes others feel when we express our gratitude for the bigger impact they have had in our lives—and overestimate how awkward it makes others feel.

In a study conducted by social psychologists Amit Kumar and Nicholas Epley, participants wrote "gratitude letters" to notable people in their lives. Some wrote letters to their parents, others to teachers or coaches, and others to friends. Before sending these letters, participants guessed how good the recipients would feel receiving these letters, as well as how awkward the other person would feel reading them. The researchers then contacted the recipients of the letters and asked them how they *actually* felt when they read the letters. As in the compliment study, participants underestimated how good it would feel— and overestimated how awkward it would feel—for the important people in their lives to receive these letters of gratitude.[3]

In another study, Kumar and Epley asked participants to think about how often they wrote these sorts of gratitude letters to other people who had impacted them: Did participants think they wrote such letters too often? Or, not often enough? Overwhelmingly, people reported feeling as if they did not write such letters often enough. It turns out, we all tend to fall short in conveying our gratitude to the very people who would most appreciate hearing it.

My husband and I are certainly not immune to this tendency. When our oldest daughter was born, she had to spend a few days in the neonatal intensive care unit (NICU) at Grand River Hospital in Kitchener, Ontario. She was fine, but it was harrowing for my husband and me to see our tiny baby hooked up to monitors and IVs. The nurses there were incredible. The care they provided not only to our daughter, but also to us, as first-time parents, was astounding. The three intense days we spent in the NICU with them served as an impromptu crash course in parenting. Once our daughter was discharged, people would comment on how comfortable we seemed changing diapers, nursing the baby, and comforting her through her first vaccines. It was the NICU nurses, we would say. They taught us so much about parenting. We told everyone how amazing our experience with these nurses had been—everyone, that is, except for them.

Three months after my daughter was discharged from the NICU, I snapped a picture of her—a beaming, smiling, healthy baby—and felt intense gratitude. I printed out the photo, wrote a message of thanks on the back, and mailed it to the nurses at the Kitchener NICU. I don't know how it ultimately made them feel to get that letter, but my hope is that it made them feel better than I imagined.

. . .

AS THESE OPENING examples reveal, we often refrain from complimenting strangers or expressing gratitude to the important people in our lives because we underestimate the impact our words have on others: how good it would make those people feel to hear the nice things we have to say. However, as I will explore in the chapters that follow, this is just one of many ways in which we underestimate our influence over others.

If you've ever felt ineffective, invisible, or inarticulate, there's a good chance you actually weren't any of those things. Those feelings may instead have been the result of a lack of awareness we all seem to have for how our words, actions, and even our mere existence affect other people: We underestimate the impact of our presence on others because we feel invisible. We refrain from asking for things because we assume others will say "no." On the other hand, we sometimes make careless, throwaway remarks because we underestimate the impact our words can have, mistakenly assuming other people will simply brush off our insensitive or inappropriate comments. And when we find ourselves in positions of power, we often fail to recognize how our innocent, half-serious suggestions can feel like commands to people with less power.

It makes sense that we would have such a lack of awareness. So much of our impact on others is unobservable or otherwise inaccessible to us. When we interact with someone and then part ways, there's usually no way for us to know how much the other person is thinking about us later. When we send a letter of gratitude, we don't tend to be there when the other person reads it. (Even if we are there, the other person doesn't typically rate for us on a standardized scale how good the letter made them feel.)

And unless you feel compelled to stand up on the subway and yell, "How many of you are looking at me right now?!," you really can't be sure how many people are watching—and are impacted by—what you are doing.

This is where research by my colleagues and me comes in. We have spent decades bringing to light the influence people have on others that they don't ordinarily get to see. We ask our participants the kinds of questions we all want to know about our own influence on others: Did he notice whether I was there today? How much did she take to heart what I said earlier? Do they know they can push back on my suggestions? Will she do this if I ask her?

People's answers to these questions have been illuminating. So often we *feel* as if we have little impact. However, the research shows that in fact people see us, listen to us, and agree to do things for us more often than we realize—for better, and worse.

Here I should probably offer a warning: This is not going to be your typical book on influence and persuasion. Conventional books on influence and persuasion generally have one goal in mind: to show you how to gain the influence you *don't* have, presumably so you will go forth and use your newly acquired influence boldly. My goal in writing this book isn't to help you gain influence, but to make you more aware of the influence you already *do* have but don't realize. Once you are aware of the influence you have, you may indeed decide to go forth and boldly use this newly discovered influence. You may be more willing to say what's on your mind and ask for what you need. Then again, you may not. Once you realize how hard it is for people to say "no" to you, or how many people are likely to take your haphazard musings seriously, you may find there are times when you'd rather take a step back and use your influence *less*.

Ultimately, I hope this book will help you to recognize the influence you have so that you can use it more mindfully. I want you to feel more emboldened to exercise your influence when it makes sense to do so, while also taking greater responsibility for the influence you may at times wield in ways you don't intend or may not even be aware. Also, I like your shirt!

YOU HAVE MORE
INFLUENCE
THAN YOU THINK

1

UNSEEN INFLUENCE

MR. MAGOO, the stubbornly near-sighted cartoon character who first graced television screens back in 1949,* is known for walking and squinting through other people's lives and causing chaos in his wake. In one *Magoo* episode, he mistakenly enters a rocket launch facility he thinks is a casino, pulls a lever he believes to be a slot machine, and through a series of convoluted errors and events, ends up launching the director of the facility into space. In another episode, he mistakes Dr. Frankenstein's laboratory for a hotel bar, and through yet another series of complicated events, ruins the diabolical experiment Frankenstein is performing on his monster.

The thing about Mr. Magoo—and the key comic device of the character—is that he is completely oblivious to the chaos he causes. As he walks through the world impacting people left and right in big getting-launched-into-space kinds of ways, he can't

---

* A time when audiences were less likely to call out the patently ableist overtones of such a character.

see past his own nose to comprehend the effect and impact he has on others, and how the behavior and attention of everyone around him has shifted because he's walked into the room.

What I hope to show throughout this book is that we've all got a little Mr. Magoo in us. As we lumber through our everyday lives, not seeing past our own noses, we leave behind our own trail of impact on the various people we encounter throughout our day. And, like Mr. Magoo, we are largely oblivious to that impact.

This revelation can be both empowering and sobering. On the one hand, it means that having influence is in many ways easier and less extraordinary than we imagine. While the times you've tried and failed to influence someone may loom large, there are undoubtedly far more examples of times you've influenced someone without trying at all—and without ever seeing the influence you had. On the other hand, this also means there have likely been times you influenced someone unintentionally, in ways you may even wish you hadn't.

As any marketing executive will tell you, the first step toward having influence is getting someone's attention—in fact, grabbing someone's attention is the hardest part of persuasion, they would likely say. In this chapter, we will turn that presupposition on its head. We will address the misperception that in order to get someone to pay attention to you, you have to wave your hands around and shout. Ad executives may need to pull out all the stops in order to grab people's attention, but you don't. You already have it. You are a person, not an ad or a tweet, and people are wired to notice other people. More than that, they are wired to wonder what other people are thinking, and to adjust their own thoughts and behaviors accordingly. What this means is that you are quietly and subtly influencing the people around you all the time—without even trying, and often without realizing it.

YOU ARE NOT AS INVISIBLE AS YOU THINK

On September 12, 2017, Ty Cobb, a lawyer who was at the time in charge of coordinating the White House's response to the Mueller investigation into former president Donald Trump's alleged entanglements with Russia, sat down for lunch with John Dowd, Trump's lead outside attorney in that same investigation. They were seated at a popular Washington, D.C., restaurant's outdoor patio adjacent to a busy sidewalk. Popular restaurant. Outdoors. Busy sidewalk. It doesn't get much more public than that. Despite this, the two attorneys proceeded to discuss for over forty-five minutes sensitive information about the ongoing investigation, including details about that surreptitious "Trump Tower meeting," Jared Kushner's precarious standing in the group, and how aggressive to be about invoking executive privilege—details the world now knows because a *New York Times* reporter happened to be sitting at the next table. That reporter, Ken Vogel, posted a photo on Twitter of the two attorneys talking with the caption, "Here's a photo of Ty Cobb & John Dowd casually & loudly discussing details of Russia investigation at @BLTSteakDC while I sat at next table."[1]

This accidental scoop became a news story about internal clashes between Trump's lawyers on how much to cooperate with the Russia inquiry. But it quickly turned into a media sensation that was less about the substance of the scoop itself, and more about how the scoop came to be. As noted by *Washington Post* reporter Fred Barbash, "It is every Washington reporter's dream to sit down at a restaurant, overhear secret stuff, and get a scoop."[2] Yet how these two individuals—and Cobb, in particular, who was brought in to "professionalize" Trump's response to the Russia inquiry—could have been so careless as to be overheard talking about such sensitive information proved a captivating mystery. Noting the proximity of the restaurant to the *New York Times*'s Washington outpost in an interview with MSNBC, Vogel said, "It's perhaps doubly astounding that they would have this conversation at this restaurant where a number of power players are known to lunch, but also reporters are known to lunch, and *Times* reporters in particular." Or, as put more succinctly by *Washington Post* columnist Dana Milbank, "What the hell was Cobb thinking?"[3]

Erica Boothby, along with Yale researchers Margaret Clark and John Bargh, may have an answer to the mystery of what Cobb was thinking, an answer that sheds light not only on the mystery of this scoop, but also on the mystery of why we often fail to recognize the impact we have on other people. According to these researchers, Cobb may simply have been exhibiting our tendency to underestimate how much we are observed by others. We tend to believe that others are watching us less, listening to us less, and generally paying less attention to us than they actually are. Boothby and her colleagues coined the term the "invisibility cloak illusion"[4] to describe the invisibility we often feel as we go about our daily lives—sitting on the train with our headphones on or walking through the park in our sunglasses,[5] all while observing the people around us yet feeling unobserved ourselves, as if we're wearing an invisibility cloak. But, as lawyers Cobb and Dowd discovered much to their chagrin, people do observe us—more than we realize.

In one of the early studies demonstrating this phenomenon, Boothby and her coauthors surveyed students who had been

dining with others in a busy campus dining hall. The researchers wanted to see whether the students felt more invisible—in
other words, less observed—than they in fact were by other people while eating lunch in a public place.

To test this hypothesis, they randomly assigned students
exiting the dining hall to different conditions. In one condition, the students were asked how much they found themselves
noticing or observing the people around them in the dining
hall (i.e., their behavior, mannerisms, and appearance), how
curious they had been about the people around them, and the
extent to which they had wondered what was going on inside
the heads of the people around them. Students assigned to
another condition were asked how much they thought the
other people in the dining hall were noticing or observing *them*
(their behavior, mannerisms, and appearance), were curious
about *them*, and wondered what was going in *their* heads. Participants' ratings of how much they found themselves observing other people were more than 67% higher than participants'
ratings of how much they thought other people were observing
them. Despite the fact that everyone is busy observing everyone else, we tend to think we are somehow more invisible than
the people around us.

Why would we think this? Let me ask you this: Have you
ever caught someone's eye, felt embarrassed that they caught
you looking, and then quickly looked away or pretended to have
been looking at something else? I'm guessing the answer is "yes,"
because that's what people do. Vision scientists even have a
name for this: "gaze deflection."[6] When we are looking at someone, we try to hide that fact. But that means the people who are
looking at you are trying to hide that fact, too. Because of that,
we're rarely confronted with evidence that we're being watched.

As we scan the world, we just see a bunch of people staring at the ceiling or their hands and fail to realize that as soon as we turn away, their eyes are on us. In fact, in another study, Boothby and her collaborators asked participants, "When you happen to make eye contact with someone you don't know, do you tend to think it's because you were looking at them, or because they were looking at you?" The vast majority of participants in this study (76%) thought the eye contact was the result of *them* looking at the stranger, which simply can't be right.

And it's not just strangers who are more curious about us than we realize. The researchers found the same thing when they used the identical cafeteria context, but asked participants how much attention they were paying and how curious they were about their own dining companions. Even our friends notice us and wonder what we're thinking more than we realize.

All of this is important for our purposes because if we don't even realize the extent to which other people notice us, how can we possibly assess the extent to which we impact other people? What I said earlier remains true—you are a person, not an ad— but one useful insight of advertising is that attention is the first step toward influence. So, the first part of underestimating our power of persuasion is underestimating how much other people pay attention to us.

NO NEED TO GET PARANOID

If when reading about the invisibility cloak illusion you thought to yourself, "Well, *I* knew everyone was looking at my [insert embarrassing personal insecurity here]," let me offer this caveat before moving on to the next section: Other people aren't paying attention to what you think they are paying attention to. Specifically, they aren't paying attention to [that embarrassing personal insecurity].

Most of us can relate to the mortifying feeling that someone has caught you looking at them (when in fact it's just as likely you caught *them* looking at *you*) described earlier. But at the same time, most of us can relate to the equally mortifying feeling that everyone is looking at your awkward cowlick, noticing that you stumbled, or staring at that weird stain on your pants. Rest assured: this has been studied scientifically, and they aren't. In a now classic experiment, social psychologists Tom Gilovich, Vicky Medvec, and Ken Savitsky tested whether our concerns that everyone is staring at the things we find most embarrassing are overblown.[7] They had groups of student participants come into the lab and randomly chose one student per session to don a T-shirt that had been deemed sufficiently embarrassing in student interviews conducted prior to the study: a Barry Manilow concert T-shirt.*

The experimenter then led the participant who had been assigned to wear this embarrassing T-shirt to another room where the rest of the experiment would purportedly take place. When the participant entered the room, they found a group of other participants already seated around a table. Just as they were about to sit down and join the group, one of the experimenters interrupted, saying that on second thought the other participants were already too far ahead in the experiment, so the participant wearing the Barry Manilow T-shirt should probably

---

* This study was conducted a few years prior to the emergence of the hipster culture that might ironically embrace such a T-shirt.

wait outside for a moment. In this moment while the participant waited outside the room, the experimenters collected two key pieces of information: One experimenter asked the participant who was wearing the T-shirt to estimate how many of the other participants noticed who was on their T-shirt; the other experimenter asked each of the other participants whether they noticed who was on that participant's T-shirt. This way, the experimenters were able to compare the percentage of people T-shirt wearers thought had noticed the embarrassing image on their T-shirt to the percentage of people who actually noticed the embarrassing image.

Here's the good news: Although the T-shirt wearers thought close to half of the people in the room had noticed their embarrassing T-shirt, only about a quarter of the people in the room actually did. In other words, T-shirt wearers thought twice as many people were paying attention to this embarrassing aspect of their appearance than were actually paying attention to it. The researchers called this finding the "spotlight effect" because, as they say, "people tend to believe that the social spotlight shines more brightly on them than it really does."

In this study, people overestimated the extent to which others were paying attention to them, but as we saw in the previous section, people also seem at times to underestimate the extent to which others pay attention to them. How can these two effects—the invisibility cloak illusion and the spotlight effect—coexist? In their discussion of the original spotlight effect findings, Gilovich and his coauthors in fact anticipated the circumstances in which their effect would likely reverse—something they referred to as a "reverse spotlight effect," and which ultimately, in the hands of other researchers, became the invisibility cloak illusion. While we tend to overestimate the extent to which other people's attention is on us when we are vividly self-conscious about something, in almost every other situation in our lives—as we are going about our daily routines, wearing our usual clothes, doing the things we do mindlessly and habitually—we tend to underestimate the extent to which other people's attention is on us.

To demonstrate this distinction, Boothby and her colleagues (the invisibility cloak researchers) ran another study, and this time they took a page from the Gilovich team's playbook.[8] Rather than surveying students in a dining hall, they recruited student participants into the lab. Upon their arrival, participants were assigned to one of two conditions. In one condition, participants were given a T-shirt to put on over their clothes. As in the spotlight effect studies, the T-shirt had a face prominently displayed on it, but since Barry Manilow T-shirts are harder to come by now than they were back in the 1990s, the face that was displayed was that of the infamous drug lord Pablo Escobar. The effect, however, was the same: participants felt self-conscious about wearing the T-shirt. In the other condition, participants simply wore the clothing they came to the experiment in—they weren't given any reason to feel especially self-conscious about their appearance.

Participants (wearing either the provided shirt or their own clothes) were then led to a waiting room where another participant was already seated, waited for five minutes, and were taken to another room to complete some questionnaires. During this time, the experimenters collected the same sort of information collected in the spotlight effect studies. They asked participants in both the "provided shirt" and "own shirt" conditions the extent to which they thought the other person in the waiting room had been noticing or thinking about their shirt, and they asked the other person in the waiting room the extent to which they had actually been noticing or thinking about the other participant's shirt.

When participants were provided with the Pablo Escobar shirt, Boothby and her colleagues replicated the spotlight effect. Participants thought the other participant had been noticing and thinking about their shirt more than they actually had been. However, when participants simply wore their own clothes and had no specific reason to be self-conscious about their shirt, they thought the other participant had been noticing and thinking about their shirt less than they actually had been. In other words, when we're feeling particularly self-conscious about something, we're so focused on it that we assume everyone else must be as well. We feel like we are in the spotlight and everyone is looking at our most embarrassing feature. But they aren't. No one else is as focused on the things we're insecure about as we are. However, when there's no reason for us to be particularly focused on what we're doing or wearing, in fact we think other people are *less* focused on it than they actually are. We may have had that shirt for years, but to someone else, it's new, and they think it's pretty cute.

The important thing, of course, isn't the fashion trend we may unwittingly inspire because people are paying more attention to our old T-shirts than we thought. It's all the other ways in which our presence can change the way other people think and feel, unbeknownst to us. Ultimately, psychologists have found that there are unseen ways in which our presence can influence the ways others see or experience something, causing them to think, feel, or act differently as a result.

YOUR PRESENCE IN OTHER
PEOPLE'S EXPERIENCES

When my husband and I started dating, he was on a mission to get me to like his favorite band. He sent me a playlist along with detailed arguments about the musical importance of each song on it, and he insisted that I listen to these songs in his meticulously curated order. So, I did. Alone in my apartment one evening, I put on my headphones, leaned back, and listened to the entire playlist exactly as instructed. It was . . . okay. As tactfully as I tried to report back my lukewarm reaction, I'll admit, he was bummed. But he eventually got over it, and we mostly didn't talk about the band after that. Until one day, many months later, we were on a road trip and he put on the same playlist. He didn't say much about it, he just casually put it on once we had lost the local radio station, but I quickly recognized the band. As we drove along side by side, gazing out the window, we listened to the entire playlist together in silence. And you know what? It was *so much better*. I started to come around on the band.

I thought of this experience when I learned about another set of studies conducted by Erica Boothby in which she and her colleagues examined how sharing an experience with another person has an impact on our own experience of that thing. Simply sitting and listening to music with someone else or standing next to someone else while staring at a painting—without talking, gesturing, or engaging in any sort of overt attempt to influence the other person—can nonetheless have an impact on the other person's experience.

Boothby and her colleagues demonstrated this effect by recruiting participants into the lab under the pretense that they would be conducting a taste test. Participants in the study were told they would be rating the flavors of two pieces of chocolate, one after the other. The twist participants were unaware of was that the two pieces of chocolate were actually taken from the same chocolate bar and should therefore have tasted exactly the same. Despite this, the researchers expected that participants would in fact rate these identically tasting chocolates differently when they were the only one tasting the chocolate as opposed to when they believed that another participant was tasting the chocolate at the same time. What these researchers ended up finding is a good excuse to order dessert on a date: When participants tasted the chocolate at the same time as another purported study participant, they said they liked the chocolate more and rated it as more flavorful than when they were the only ones eating the chocolate.[9]

Before we get ahead of ourselves in assuming the way to get someone to like anything is simply to share the experience with them, I should note that Boothby and colleagues didn't just find that sharing experiences with other people made them more pleasant. Instead, they found that sharing experiences amplified them. In this case, the pleasant experience of eating sweet chocolate was amplified. But in another study, they found that unpleasant experiences can similarly be amplified. In a follow-up study, Boothby and colleagues used the same experimental setup, but they had participants taste extremely bitter chocolate that they had confirmed through pretesting people found highly unpleasant. It turned out that tasting this unpleasant chocolate with someone else didn't make the experience more pleasant—rather, it made it even more unpleasant. Sharing the experience simply made it more intense.

Importantly, the researchers in these studies took pains to ensure that there was no communication between the two individuals. They were aware of one another's presence, but there was no comparing of notes, no eye contact, and no gesturing. So, how is it that your experience of eating a piece of chocolate can change so dramatically—in one case from an average of 5.5 to an average of 7 out of 10 on a scale of liking—just because you are sharing it with another person?

One particularly intriguing theory offered by the researchers is that this occurs through a process called mentalization. If we know someone else is doing the same thing as us (like eating chocolate), while we are experiencing the deliciousness of the chocolate, we are also simultaneously imagining how the other person is experiencing the deliciousness of the chocolate. It is deliciousness, squared.

Other research conducted by psychologist Garriy Shteynberg and colleagues finds that our minds do indeed seem to go into overdrive in this manner when we believe we are evaluating something others are also simultaneously evaluating. If you know that other members of your social group are reading the same book or watching the same show as you, you tend to pay more attention to, better remember aspects of, and more carefully evaluate that book or show as you try to figure out your group's opinion of it (i.e., What do "we" think about this?). The extra mental energy you expend as you do so can in turn influence your own attitude about whatever it is you are assessing, even without any explicit discussion of or knowledge about other people's opinions.

In a series of studies, when participants were led to believe they were evaluating a set of paintings at the same time as other participants with whom they shared some commonalities, they wrote more complex descriptions of the paintings. Additionally, their evaluations of the paintings became more extreme than when they believed they were the only ones evaluating the paintings, or that others were evaluating a different set of paintings.[10] The extra attention and consideration participants gave to objects they believed others like them were also evaluating intensified participants' attitudes toward those objects, just like mentalizing about someone else's experience of a piece of chocolate intensifies the experience of eating that chocolate.

Mentalizing is something we do instinctively when we are around other people. We are naturally curious about other people, and we try to figure out what is going on in their heads—how they are thinking about and reacting to something. The thing to keep in mind for the purposes of this book is that other people are doing this to us, too. When we are around other people, they are also busy trying to figure out what's going on in *our* heads. And, as we saw earlier in this chapter, they do this to a greater extent than we realize. This means that not only do people notice our presence more than we realize, but they also see what we are doing, and wonder why we are doing it and what we are thinking; this process of trying to understand what we are doing can cause them to think and feel differently in our presence. Not only does this process affect how other people experience the world when we're around, it can also change their minds.

THE POWER OF BEING IN THE AUDIENCE

When I applied to graduate school, one of the places I applied was the Psychology Department at my undergraduate alma mater, Brown University (now the Department of Cognitive, Linguistic, and Psychological Sciences). I was fortunate enough to be accepted there, and subsequently received a lovely email from one of my former professors saying that she remembered me from a class I had taken with her years before. The class she was referring to was mostly lecture, which means that I sat somewhere in the rows of seats populated by more than fifty other students, likely somewhere closer to the back than the front. I'm sure I listened intently and nodded as she spoke, but I am equally sure that I never said a thing, since I was far too nervous to speak up in class back then. And yet, she remembered me.

Now that I teach my own large lecture course of 200 students, I find the fact that she remembered my face out of a sea of other faces much less surprising than I did back then. When you are sitting in a crowd, it is easy to feel invisible—to assume that even as you stare intently at the person at the front of the room, that person isn't looking back at you. But they are. Trust me, I see my students doing all sorts of things I'm sure they think I don't see.

Performers, too, have many exasperating stories about the behavior of audience members who simply assumed the person on the stage wasn't paying attention to them. My cousin, Erika Rauer, was an opera singer for many years. She recounted to me how difficult it was to avoid getting distracted during auditions in front of audience members who would do things like, say, eat their lunch loudly, crumple up their paper bag, and then throw it at a wastebasket across the room. (Despite being in the middle of a performance, she was so aware of this behavior she even recalls that this person missed the trash can—which, clearly, serves them right.) Tony award–winning Broadway superstar Patti LuPone made headlines a few years ago for losing patience with an audience member who was staring at her phone for the entire performance; finally, she reached down and snatched the phone out of the audience member's hands.[11]

Does all of this mean your favorite boy band member is

singing only to you as you look up adoringly from the crowd? Probably not. (Sorry!) But it is a valuable illustration of an under-appreciated aspect of influence: it is a two-way street. We tend to think of the person at the front of the room, the one doing most of the talking, as the person with all the power and influence. But as the uniquely insightful comedian Hannah Gadsby, of the acclaimed Netflix special *Nanette* (and her hilarious follow-up *Douglas*), puts it, it's not the case that just because someone's "got the magic stick that amplifies their voice ... everyone has to listen."[12]

In fact, the person in the front of the room has the same concerns as anyone else—they want to know what people think of them, want to be liked, and want to feel effective. How do they accomplish all that? They do it by paying attention to their audience, checking in with their audience, and, in large part, by telling their audience what they want to hear.

Comedians, like Gadsby, are well-known for tailoring their sets to their audiences' tastes. Marina Franklin, who created the comedy special *Single Black Female,* has said of figuring out which of her jokes are funny, "I don't know until I get in front of an audience."[13] Jerry Seinfeld, in the documentary *Comedian*, says to an audience he is testing new material out on, "Can you believe you're in charge of deciding whether our brilliant ideas are good or not?"[14]

Craving the approval of one's audience is not specific to comedians or, as we'll discuss next, politicians. It is human nature. That, in turn, gives audiences an awful lot of power. Simply by listening intently to what someone says—by being an engaged audience—we can have an impact on how a speaker decides to talk about an issue. And, ultimately, that can change what a speaker ends up believing about that issue.

Think of the extreme rhetoric so many supposedly power-ful influencers will use in front of receptive audiences—rhetoric they are quick to tone down in less sympathetic contexts. How many headlines have been made by politicians pandering to their base by making avowals that other audiences might find reprehensible? At an LGBT-for-Hillary fundraising gala in 2016, Hillary Clinton referenced half of Trump supporters as a "basket of deplorables."[15] In 2012, at a $50,000-a-plate fundraiser hosted by a hedge fund manager, Mitt Romney made comments dis-missing 47% of the American population as "believing they are victims."[16] Would either of them have used this same rhetoric in front of a more general audience? Unlikely. Indeed, both were quick to rephrase their comments once the media picked up on them—and broadcasted them to a wider audience.

As with comedians, it is easy to dismiss this kind of pander-ing from politicians. After all, they have concrete incentives—they're trying to drum up support and votes from whomever is in their immediate vicinity. However, these are just extreme exam-ples of an ordinary human behavior. Everyone phrases things in ways they think will appeal to their audience, whether address-ing a roomful of strangers or chatting one-on-one with a close friend. We state our opinion a bit more extremely to a friend who we know agrees with us, and a little less so to a stranger whose opinion we don't yet know. Psychologists call this "audience tun-ing."[17] People naturally tune their messages to their audience for all types of reasons ranging from the pragmatic to the affiliative to the self-serving.

Even when we have no ulterior motive, we engage in audience tuning. To give a classic example, random strangers approached for directions on the streets of Boston gave longer, more detailed directions to someone with a rural Missourian accent than to someone with a local Boston accent.[18] At first glance, this may seem obvious. Of course, people would give more detailed directions to someone from out of town. But let's reflect for a moment on the complexity of this behavior. As Bob Krauss, a psycholinguist and social psychologist emeritus at Columbia, points out, this behavior requires three discrete actions: first, assigning the person asking for directions to a relevant social category ("local" vs. "out-of-towner") based on a single piece of information (their accent), then inferring the set of knowledge and beliefs that a person from that social category is likely to hold (Do they know "Mass Ave"?), and finally coming up with a message that would make sense to that person based on those assumptions ("You'll see Massachusetts Avenue on your right").[19] Yet we do this regularly without a second thought—simply to ensure our audience understands what we are saying.

Of course, we also tune our messages to our audience for other reasons, a major one being that we want people to like us (or laugh at our jokes or vote for us). It isn't exactly social psychology's most surprising finding—although it is one of its most reliable findings—that people tend to like others with similar views.[20] On some level, we all seem to know this to be true. For that reason, we tune our messages not only to reflect the presumed knowledge of our audience, but also the presumed opinions of our audience. If I know the restaurant I had dinner at last night is your favorite, I'm more likely to talk about the positives of the meal than I might be if I knew you didn't like it that much. After all, we all want to be liked, and establishing common interests is one way to accomplish that goal.

In a classic study illustrating this effect, participants summarized a speech about the pros and cons of legalizing marijuana to an individual whom they knew was either for or against legalization. The speech they listened to was decidedly neutral. Yet, participants who summarized the speech for someone who was anti-legalization said the speech made a stronger case against legalization than those who summarized the speech for someone who was pro-legalization.[21] Notably, everyone in the study presumably knew that the participants weren't giving their own opinions. They were only summarizing someone else's take. Yet despite the fact that there was no implication that the opinion they were offering was their own, participants still tuned their messages in ways they thought would please their audience. It is easy to see from this study how information—e.g., polling information or the findings of an investigation—can get distorted for the purposes of making it more palatable to whatever audience it is being conveyed.

"A BIT THAT CRUSHED"

We now know that part of an audience's unseen power is that audiences can shape the very messages they receive via their presumed knowledge, beliefs, and opinions. But the power of the audience goes further than that. Audiences don't just influence the messages to which they are exposed, they also influence the beliefs of the messengers who convey them. You may think that when people engage in audience tuning of this sort, it's simply pandering—it's not like they actually believe what they are saying. While it's true they may not start out believing what they say, it turns out, once they say it, they do kind of start to believe it.

When Trevor Noah, host of the *The Daily Show*, was a guest on *Late Night with Seth Meyers* back in 2017, the two comedians joked about the ways in which Donald Trump's rhetoric started out as a means of indulging his base, but subsequently morphed into some of his die-hard platforms: "'Build the wall' was just a bit that crushed, and now he realizes he needs to, like, build a wall."[22] As absurd as that might seem, it is an extreme version of what does happen. A speaker says something to appeal to their audience, the audience reacts enthusiastically, and the speaker walks away having convinced themselves of what they said as much as anyone else.

My PhD advisor, Tory Higgins, a social psychologist at Columbia, has conducted some of the best-known studies of this phenomenon, appropriately known as the "saying-is-believing effect." In one study, known around our lab as the "Donald study,"* participants were given a description of a fictional person named Donald whose traits could be described either positively or negatively—it was completely ambiguous.[23] For example, Donald was described as feeling like he didn't need to rely on anyone. From that description, you could call Donald independent (a more positive interpretation). Or, you could call him aloof (a more negative interpretation). Donald was also described as rarely changing his mind once he made it up. Based on that description, you could call Donald persistent. Or, you could call him stubborn. All told, one would be equally justified in describing Donald as independent, persistent, confident, and trustful—or as aloof, stubborn, conceited, and gullible.

After reading these ambiguous descriptions, participants were asked to summarize Donald's personality characteristics to someone who either liked or disliked him. Given the audience tuning work described earlier, it shouldn't be surprising to learn

---

* The choice of name was purely coincidental. This study was conducted in the 1970s, many years before its relevance to Donald Trump would become apparent.

that when summarizing Donald's personality traits to someone participants thought liked him, they used more positive descriptions than when summarizing the same information to someone they thought disliked him.

The interesting piece this study adds to the puzzle is that the researchers then asked participants what they thought of Donald after communicating this information. Despite the fact that everyone had read the exact same ambiguous description, participants who described Donald to someone who liked him rated him as more likable than participants who described him to someone who disliked him. And this effect persisted two weeks later when the experimenters brought participants back to the lab and once again asked them what they thought of Donald.

Just think about that for a moment. These participants were given completely neutral information. Yet they left the lab with a clear opinion—one that persisted for weeks. Furthermore, this was not because anyone tried to convince them of what a jerk Donald was—they were the ones doing all the communicating, after all. It was simply because they had an idea of what their audience wanted to hear, tailored their message to suit their audience, and then fell for their own message.

Think of what this means for traditional ideas about power and influence. People often talk about "having someone's ear" as a form of influence. But let's turn this around and ask, who has your ear? Who is tailoring their messages to what you care about? Because that can be just as important.

Harnessing the power of being in the audience can be an effective—and underappreciated—influence strategy. By inviting people to speak to you, you acquire the power that comes with being *their* audience—of making them win you over, and potentially convincing themselves along the way.

The rich and powerful already use this strategy. Hillary Clinton may have caught flak for comments she made during her presidential run, but it is the Wall Street banks and powerful government contractors that paid her $200K–$600K speaking fees who are the ones that truly know how to harness the power of being in the audience. Leaked transcripts of speeches Clinton gave to organizations like Goldman Sachs show how she tuned her message to appeal to her audience, using "far softer language than Clinton uses on the campaign trail" to reference reform legislation that was unpopular on Wall Street.[24] Much of the criticism Clinton faced for those speeches during her subsequent White House bid centered on the large sums she was paid for her appearances—the thought being that accepting such large fees would make her beholden to those organizations' interests. However, based on everything we've talked about, the strategy of paying someone to speak to you who is, or may one day be, in a position of power goes beyond mere tit for tat. It is a way to get them to consider your perspective, talk your talk, and adjust their stated position to be a little closer to yours. And in so doing, it is also a way to get them to shift their actual opinion to be a little closer to yours.

WE COPY WHAT WE SEE

One of my daughter's favorite books is *The Curious Garden* by Peter Brown. It's the story of a boy named Liam who finds a neglected garden in a gray and dreary city and begins quietly and unassumingly tending to it. For most of the book, the only character we see is Liam: Liam discovering the garden; Liam pruning the plants; Liam walking to the garden to care for it day after day. The story unfolds in such a way that we never really stop to wonder what others think of Liam's comings and goings—much as we might not think much about whether other people are paying attention to ours.

Over time, Liam's garden grows and spreads. His plants start popping up in unexpected places—little oases of color and life. In a tiny way, Liam's efforts have begun to transform the city. The story could easily end there. It would be enough to celebrate Liam's efforts and the small impact they have had in breaking up the bleak landscape. But the story continues, and near the end of the book, we realize we are not the only ones who have been watching Liam's labor of love. As we zoom out from our close study of Liam, we see a line of children walking behind him, carrying watering cans and gardening tools as they venture off to tend to their own budding gardens. Not only had Liam's garden spread beyond what he could have imagined, but the very act of gardening had as well. As Brown writes, "the most surprising things that popped up were the new gardeners."[25]

The last page of the book depicts the same overhead view of Liam's city the book opens with, but it has now been completely transformed from a gray, industrial, lifeless image to a city full of lush green space. Liam's garden is just a tiny piece of this new landscape. In the grand scheme of things, the direct impact of his efforts on the city was really quite small. But the indirect impact of his behavior—the way his behavior spread to others, and the resulting collective effort—was exponentially larger.

This phenomenon of a behavior spreading from one person to another like an infectious disease is known as "behavioral contagion." It's a concept that has been written about for centuries, as scholars have observed "outbreaks" of eating habits, styles, and even suicides across various populations and attributed these outbreaks to the human tendency to mimic what we see.

While a disease metaphor is useful for illustrative purposes, the way behaviors actually spread from person to person tends to be more complex.[26] Diseases can spread from a single exposure to an infected person you don't know—a process known as "simple contagion." However, you're unlikely to "catch" a potentially risky or expensive behavior, like installing solar panels on your home, from a stranger on the bus. These types of behaviors typically take multiple exposures, especially to people within your close social network. Which is why, although you might be unlikely to catch the desire to install a solar panel from a stranger on the bus, you might actually catch such an urge from your neighbor.

Robert Frank, an economist at Cornell and author of *Under the Influence: Putting Peer Pressure to Work*, among other books, has written extensively about the importance of tapping into this form of behavioral contagion to address social problems such as climate change. According to Frank, certain climate-friendly behaviors are "particularly contagious," and one of his favorite examples of this is the installation of solar panels. As Frank points out, "Each new installation in a neighborhood can, over time, lead to several additional ones."[27] Aerial imagery even offers a visual demonstration of the contagiousness of solar panels, showing how houses with solar panels tend to be clustered near one another.

What the phenomenon of behavioral contagion means for you and the influence you have is that each action you take—whether you are installing a solar panel or hosting a destination wedding—actually has two effects. One effect is direct. When you install a solar panel, it has the direct effect of reducing your own carbon footprint; on the other hand, when you invite a hundred people to fly to Hawaii for your wedding, you are also directly responsible for the carbon emissions required to get them there. But the direct effects of these actions are in fact quite small. Any one solar panel or any one wedding is really just a drop in the bucket. That fact can feel frustrating when you're trying to make a change for good. Alternatively, it can make you think, "Why not?" when considering the potential negative impact of one individual choice in the grand scheme of things.

However, it is perhaps more important to consider the second, and exponentially larger, *indirect* effect of your actions. When you install a solar panel, yes, you shrink your own personal carbon footprint. But more than that, you also increase the likelihood that other people in your neighborhood will follow suit and install their own solar panels.[28] When you host a destination wedding, that one decision is a relatively trivial indulgence in carbon terms. But when you consider that your decision to do so increases the likelihood that others in your social circle will choose to have destination weddings, which in turn increases the likelihood that attendees of those weddings will have destination weddings and so on, that decision begins to seem less trivial. By taking into consideration the potential outbreak of behaviors that our own individual actions have the potential to spark, our seemingly inconsequential individual choices start to feel more consequential, for better and worse.

Yet it is precisely these indirect, more consequential effects of our own actions that we are most likely to overlook. As we've seen throughout this chapter, we tend to underestimate the extent to which people notice, pay attention to, and are genuinely curious about our thoughts and behaviors. That means we are likely to underestimate the extent to which our neighbors will, for example, notice the solar panel that just popped up in our backyard like one of Liam's plants, wonder how we came to the decision to put it up, begin to mentally simulate that decision process themselves, and start to shift toward considering such a decision for themselves. In other words, we may underestimate the biggest part of our influence—the indirect impact of our actions, through other people's tendency to see and copy them.

IT'S WORTH SHOWING UP

We are instinctively attuned to other people—we notice them, remember them, wonder what is going on in their minds, tune our thoughts and messages to them, and copy their behavior. But that means other people are also attuned to us and exhibit the same behaviors toward us. When we think about how much influence we have, the first mistake we make is underestimating how much other people pay attention to us. By showing you a few ways in which your mere presence changes the way the people around you think, feel, and act, without you even knowing, I hope I have disabused you of that notion.

Ultimately, what this suggests is that just by being present—by "coming to the table," so to speak—you can have a big impact on other people, even if you never say a word. For example, at my university, we go through various academic reviews to keep up with the times and identify changes worth making to our programs that might benefit students and faculty. As part of these reviews, we have numerous meetings, and faculty are invited to come offer their suggestions and join in the discussion. Not surprisingly, the cohort that tends to be most represented—and most dominant—in these meetings are older, established faculty. After all, they are the ones who feel like they have something to contribute. And to be clear, they do. They've been there a long time and have often held leadership positions at the university. They've seen what's worked and what hasn't, understand the big picture, and can anticipate the unintended consequences of well-meaning suggestions.

But here's the thing: The recommendations that come out of these meetings don't just impact established, tenured faculty. They also affect junior, untenured faculty—those who wonder if it's even worth coming to these meetings because they think they won't have anything to contribute. And oftentimes, they might not. They're often still learning about the problems that need to be addressed, so they certainly aren't expected to have all the solutions. So, does it really make a difference when junior faculty show up if they don't end up saying much?

Yes! As we have seen, just being present in the room can make a huge difference because your presence—as both speaker *and* audience—can affect others. Others see you, tune their messages to you, and think about how you are reacting to what's being said. And all of this may ultimately change how they think and feel about the issues. When you have ideas and thoughts, you should voice them (more about that in the next chapter). But when you don't, you can still make a difference simply by being part of the audience. So, next time you're unsure whether to attend something, remember what we learned in this chapter, and show up. You may end up influencing the discussions people have and the decisions they make for the better, even if you don't say a thing.

2

YOUR POWER OF PERSUASION

WHO DO YOU THINK goes to more parties, you or other people? Who has more friends? Who has a wider social network? Who sees and interacts with their family more? Who is closer to the "inner circle" of your social group?

Sebastian Deri, a social psychologist at Cornell University, in collaboration with fellow psychologists Shai Davidai and Tom Gilovich, asked more than 3,000 participants across eleven studies these very questions.[1] Study participants were shoppers in a mall, college students on campus, and online survey respondents. In some studies, the average participant was nineteen years old, in others the average participant was thirty-seven years old. In each of these demographically diverse samples, people reported believing, on average, that they went to fewer parties, had fewer friends, dined out less, saw their extended family less, and were further removed from the "inner circle" or "in-crowd" than their peers. In other words, college students living on campus away from their parents, surrounded by co-eds and fraternities, believed themselves to be less socially active

29

than their peers. At the same time, adults in their mid-to-late thirties juggling work and family also believed that *they* were less socially active than *their* peers.

For a long time, it seemed as if researchers were constantly uncovering new ways in which people were overconfident. We now know the average person thinks they are more athletic,[2] moral,[3] creative,[4] and a better driver[5] than the average person (which, I must point out, is not possible by definition). However, in contrast to the long list of contexts in which people have been shown to display overconfidence, in recent years research has been converging around a very different conclusion when it comes to our beliefs about our proficiency for things like, say, winning friends and influencing people.

When interpreting Deri's findings, one thing we can be sure of is that the average person does *not* have a below-average social life. That would be as illogical a conclusion as the one reached by all those "above-average" drivers out there on the road—just in the opposite direction. Clearly, people are making some sort of error when assessing their own social prowess. But if people think they are more intelligent, more moral, more creative, and better drivers than average—that is, if we tend to be *overconfident* in all of those other contexts—why would we be *underconfident* in this one?

Deri and colleagues explain this by describing who and what is most salient when we reflect on where we fit within a normal distribution of these categories of behavior. If, for example, I ask you how good a driver you are, you will most likely look inward to your own experiences with driving. You will think of your last time behind the wheel and recall how you bravely and steadily navigated the [insert that road with all the reckless drivers in your area here]. And you would firmly pat yourself on the back, confident in all that above-average driving you were doing.

Indeed, when Deri and his colleagues asked participants how they would answer a series of nonsocial questions, such as how they would determine whether the size of their vocabulary (rather than their social network) was smaller or larger than others, and whether they cooked (rather than dined out) more or less than others, they said that in order to answer these questions they would be more likely to look inward to their own traits, abilities, and behaviors. And it turns out that participants in Deri's studies also displayed the typical overconfidence effect for these nonsocial questions—for example, they thought they had larger-than-average vocabularies and cooked more often than other people.

On the other hand, if I ask you about your social life, your attention will most likely be directed outward to the social lives of others. After all, other people are a critical part of the whole concept of being social. Indeed, this is how Deri's participants said they would answer the specifically social sorts of questions at the beginning of this section. In order to determine the relative size of their social network and frequency of dining out, for example, participants said they would be more likely to look outward to other people's traits, behaviors, and abilities.

Importantly, however, the people we compare ourselves to when we engage in such an exercise aren't just any people. They are the people who come to mind most easily when we consider what it means to be social. In other words, when evaluating our own social lives, we tend to conjure up and compare ourselves to *exemplars* of sociability who, by definition, are exceptionally social. We think of the people who were partying down the hall when we were studying alone in our dorm room, or the people whose photos of concerts and parties we scroll through while we are curled up on the couch. At the same time, we don't think of the dozen or so other students who were also trying to study in their dorm rooms in that same hall that night, or all the other homebodies scrolling through other people's photos at the same time we are. Therefore, we think that we are less sociable than the average person because we don't actually compare ourselves to the average person—we compare ourselves to the prototypical social butterfly.

All of this is important for our purposes because these same comparisons factor into our evaluations of our own power of persuasion. When we try to assess the amount of influence we have, we tend to think of social media influencers, trendsetters, gurus, power brokers—exemplars of what it means to have influence. And when we inevitably fail to stack up against these prototypical influencers, we conclude that we are subpar. But just like not getting an invitation to the Met Gala doesn't mean you have an inferior social life, not having a tweet that goes viral or not having 100,000 followers on Instagram doesn't mean you are an inferior influencer. Because most people *weren't* invited to the Met Gala. Most tweets *don't* go viral. And most people *don't* have 100,000 Instagram followers.

What this also suggests is that another way in which we have more influence than we realize is that we are more socially connected than we realize. In other words, you have more reach, in marketing speak, than you think. This is true not only in "real life," but also on social media. A graph from 2013 entitled, "You're a bigger deal on Twitter than you think," depicts an analysis of the number of followers per Twitter account and finds that the median Twitter account has sixty-one followers (after eliminating any accounts that hadn't tweeted in the month prior, which, when included, bring the median down to one follower).[6] There are, indeed, a substantial number of accounts with tens or hundreds of thousands of followers, or more. If a Twitter user with, say, a respectable 1,000 followers were to compare themselves to those accounts, of course their influence would feel inconsequential. But, in fact, back in 2013 when the analysis was done, an account with 1,000 followers would have been in the *top 4%* of Twitter users based on followers.*

These analyses don't really get at social media users' psychological experience of their own influence, however, so my graduate student Sangah Bae and I ran a couple of studies to do just that. Drawing from Deri's methods, we asked a sample of college students, and, later, a sample of working adults, "Who has more influence, friends/followers, and engagements—you, or others completing this survey?" for a group of different social media sites: Facebook, Instagram, Twitter, Snapchat, LinkedIn, and TikTok. What we found mirrored Deri and colleagues' findings: The average person in our studies thought they had less influence on social media than the average person in our studies.

Recent research has begun to converge on the idea that we are in fact underconfident when assessing personal qualities such as our social connectedness, and as we will see next, our likeability. Not only does this bias help to maintain a thriving self-improvement industry, it also suggests that we may regularly

---

* Since 2013 may seem like ancient history in Twitter years, it's worth noting that a more recent analysis tells a similar story, although it breaks the data down differently: An analysis of Twitter data conducted by Stefan Wojcik and Adam Hughes of the Pew Research Center in 2019 found that the top 10% most prolific tweeters had a median of just 386 followers ("Sizing Up Twitter Users," April 24, 2019, https://www.pewresearch.org/internet/2019/04/24/sizing-up-twitter-users/).

underestimate our own power of persuasion. Somewhat ironically, as will we see later in this chapter, this can lead us to use overly aggressive tactics in order to gain the influence we don't realize we already have.

THEY LIKE YOU. THEY REALLY LIKE YOU.

Academia has some practices that are borderline torturous for the introverted, which many academics, myself included, tend to be. One such practice is the academic talk. You might be thinking: Of course, giving a talk in front of a room full of your peers and respected senior colleagues would make anyone jittery. However, the actual talk is often the least nerve-wracking part. The talk is typically well-rehearsed, the norms of what is expected from the speaker and the audience are fairly well-established, and you generally have presentation slides to lean on.

What's always been most intimidating—at least for me—is what happens before and after the talk. The idea behind inviting a fellow researcher out for a campus visit is to get to know them and their research—but it's also for *them* to get to know all the people in the host department and *their* research. So, to give everyone a chance to get to know one another, speakers will generally spend all day before and after their talks in back-to-back, one-on-one meetings with the individual faculty members of a given department. You are escorted to an office, say hello, sit down, and converse for thirty minutes; then you are escorted to the next office, say hello, sit down, converse for another thirty minutes; and repeat. It's basically academic speed dating, all day long.

Unlike the talk, the norms of these one-on-one conversations—most often with people you don't know very well—are not so well-defined. I have spent my time in these meetings talking about everything from research to family to professional gossip to religion to David Bowie. It's a shy person's worst nightmare: forced conversation with someone you don't know in an evaluative context with hardly any guidelines regarding what counts as an appropriate conversation topic. And doing it over, and over, again.

It's not surprising that these speed-dating-style conversations can feel sort of awkward at the start. But it's more surprising to learn that they ultimately turn out to be quite enjoyable. What we realize when we've gone through enough of these kinds of rapid-fire forced conversations is that no matter how much you might think you talked too much, or weren't witty enough, or said something weird or wrong or stupid, on the whole, people walk away from these conversations feeling good about the interaction and positively toward you.

This isn't just a peculiarity of academic campus visits or forced interactions more generally. Anytime you walk away from a conversation and begin a postmortem analysis of everything you said wrong or how awkward you were, you are probably being unnecessarily harsh on yourself. We regularly make better, less awkward impressions on other people than we think we do. However, since we rarely get insight into what other people thought of us once we part ways after a conversation, we rarely have the opportunity to have our worries assuaged about the negative impressions we *think* we've made. Luckily, we can once again thank Erica Boothby, along with her collaborators Gus Cooney, Gillian Sandstrom, and Margaret Clark, for this insight via their discovery of a phenomenon they call the "liking gap."[7]

These researchers used a simple method: They invited pairs of participants who didn't know each other into the lab and instructed them to have a five-minute conversation. To make it easier for everyone, they didn't just leave participants to their own devices. They gave participants a sheet of icebreaker questions such as, "Where are you from?" and "What are your hobbies?" and told them to take turns asking one another these questions. This should have stacked the deck against the researchers' predictions, since participants didn't have to do many of the things that can make real-world conversations awkward, such as coming up with a topic to talk about or navigating awkward silences. So, on the whole, participants should have felt pretty good about their conversational skills.

However, that's not what the research team found when they had each participant go into a separate room to complete a post-conversation survey with questions about how much they liked the other person (e.g., "I would like to interact with the other participant again"; "I could see myself becoming friends with the other participant") and how much they thought the other person liked *them* (e.g., "The other participant would like to interact with me again"; "The other person could see him/herself becoming friends with me"). It turns out, for the average study participant, the person you just interacted with liked you more than you thought. The ratings participants provided of how much they liked their conversation partner were significantly higher—12.5% higher—than the ratings they provided of how much they thought their conversation partner liked them.

In follow-up studies, the researchers allowed participants to chat for as long as forty-five minutes (and some did chat for that long), to see whether the liking gap persisted even for longer conversations. It turns out, it does. Whether you're chatting with someone in line at the grocery store checkout for just a couple of minutes or trying to fill a full thirty minutes of professional banter with a colleague, the other person typically walks away from that conversation liking you more than you think.

These researchers also discovered a couple of interesting additional details about the effect. First, they found, not surprisingly, that people who are more shy display a larger liking gap. So, if you're particularly anxious about socializing, you're already doing *much* better than you think.

Second, they found that third-party observers who watched videos of pairs of participants interacting could actually tell how much the two individuals liked one another. It turns out that neutral observers are able to pick up on subtle cues two people send to one another indicating that they like each other, something participants themselves seem to miss. As the researchers explain, conversations are emotionally and cognitively demanding. When you're an active part of the conversation, you're focused on how you're coming across and are busy planning what to say next. As a result, you may miss the signals your partner is sending you telling you they think you're swell. But to someone who is just sitting back watching it happen, all those positive signals are unmistakable.

This is important for understanding the influence we have because a key takeaway from research on influence and persuasion is that people are more persuaded by people they like. In fact, Robert Cialdini, author of *Influence*, made this one of his six principles of persuasion: The Liking Principle.[8] If someone we think is really cool and interesting says we should check out a new podcast they're listening to, we're more likely to go and check it out than if someone we don't like as much says the same thing. It's an important, if not an especially surprising, principle. But that means that part of determining how much influence you have over other people is determining how much other people like you. And, as we've just seen, that's something we're not so great at. People like you more than you realize, which in turn means you have more influence than you realize.

One consequence of underestimating how much people like us is that we think people are going to be more resistant to hearing what we have to say than they actually are. We brace ourselves for a fight, obsess over exactly what to say, pile on the facts, and shout from the rooftops, when in reality, as we'll see in the next sections, we could probably take it down a few notches.

WHY YOU ARE TOO WORRIED ABOUT SAYING THE WRONG THING

In this age of constant moral outrage, it's hard not to feel wary of expressing our opinions. We assume everyone around us is dissecting our every word, ready to pounce and take up arms against whatever it is we have to say. While it's undeniable that this has been happening with increasing frequency, largely as a result of social media—which, as Yale psychology professor Molly Crockett has pointed out, systematically incentivizes moral outrage[9]—it simply isn't the case in everyday life. People generally aren't dissecting your every word, ready to pounce. In fact, research shows that people are inclined to agree—not to disagree—with what you have to say.

The first thing to know is that people simply aren't listening to or remembering most of what you say. People are, as psychologists like to say, "cognitive misers." We do the bare minimum to be able to navigate the world effectively, and we only think about things carefully if we absolutely need to or are particularly motivated to. By some researchers' calculations, people actually only remember about 10% of what you say to them, even in the moments immediately following a conversation,[10] and what they do remember tends to be the gist, or general idea, of what you said, not what you actually said.[11] But rather than taking that as an indication that you need to work harder than you thought to influence someone, in many cases this actually means you can stop worrying so much about saying the exact right thing—while still having influence.

For example, as many a teenager has gleefully discovered when asking to stay out past curfew while their parent was distracted on the phone, people will often process—and go along with—what we say mindlessly. Take this classic study by Harvard psychologist Ellen Langer and her colleagues: These researchers had people ask to cut in line in front of other people who were waiting to use the copy machine at the university library.[12] In one condition, they offered the people in line a logical reason for why they needed to cut: "Excuse me. I have five pages. May I use the Xerox machine, because I'm in a rush?" Fair enough, this person is in a rush, why not let them cut? And, indeed, 94% of people agreed to let the individual cut in front of them. By the way, if you think that's a high number (it is!) we'll return to that in the next chapter.

In another condition, however, the person asked to cut in line because they "need[ed] to make some copies"—an argument that made no sense. Everyone in line was there because they needed to make copies. Yet, practically the same proportion of people—93%—agreed to this nonsensical request. (I agreed to something similar once when I was seated at a crowded bar in Manhattan and a young couple came up to me. One of them said, "Could my girlfriend have your seat? She might be pregnant." I promptly hopped up and gave her my seat before fully processing the request. *Might* be pregnant. Wait—what? That doesn't even make sense.)

Langer and her colleagues called this "the mindlessness of ostensibly thoughtful action";[13] Robert Cialdini has called it the "click, whir . . ." response.[14] Both get at the fundamental idea that people don't process the substantive information in their environment as carefully as we might think, and a lot of influence happens without people's careful consideration of the facts.

Even when explicitly instructed to remember the precise details of an argument, it turns out people aren't the savvy skeptics waiting to shout "gotcha!" that we sometimes imagine them to be. For example, in another study, Anne Britt, a cognitive psychologist at Northern Illinois University, and her colleagues presented participants with different arguments, such as "Recycling should be federally mandated because it helps to protect the environment," or "Recycling is very beneficial because it helps to protect the environment," and asked them to remember the *precise claim* being made.[15] Now the substantive difference between claiming that something is beneficial and claiming that it should be mandated by the government is huge. Yet, many participants failed to differentiate between these two claims. They could recall that the gist of the argument was that recycling was good (almost everyone got that part right), but many couldn't recall the exact claim being made.

Not only that, but in another study by Britt and another colleague,[16] participants who were explicitly instructed to do so couldn't differentiate between arguments that made logical sense and those that were in fact nonsensical—for example, the argument that the death penalty is *immoral* because many people sentenced to death have been found innocent using DNA versus the argument that the death penalty is *ineffective* because many people sentenced to death have been found innocent using DNA*—because they were processing these arguments on a gist level. They were thinking about the argument as simply being about why the death penalty was bad, not the precise kind of bad that was being claimed (immoral vs. ineffective).

Britt and her colleagues attribute their findings to a theory known as "fuzzy-trace theory,"[17] which was developed by Cornell neuroscientist Valerie Reyna. The idea is that when we encounter a piece of information, we process it in two ways. In one area of the brain, we process and remember what was said verbatim. However, in a different area of our brain, we simultaneously process and remember something else—we remember the gist of what was said. True to the name, we encode a "fuzzy trace" of the actual message. The important thing to note, however, is that while we initially encode both the details and the gist of what was said, the memory for verbatim information fades quite quickly, while the memory of the gist—the message's fuzzy trace—lasts much longer.

Thus, for example, if you were to make an impromptu impassioned—but rambling, and possibly logically inconsistent— speech about why *Buffy the Vampire Slayer* is the best show ever (which, to be clear, it is), the people who hear this speech will eventually forget the logical inconsistencies and remember only

---

* The first argument is logically coherent (whether you agree with it or not). If I've claimed that the death penalty is immoral and supported that claim by saying many sentenced to death have been found innocent, the logical connection between these two things (what linguists refer to as the "warrant") is that something that leads to the death of innocent people is immoral. However, the second argument has no such logical connection. If I've claimed that the death penalty is ineffective and supported that claim by saying many sentenced to death have been found innocent, what is the warrant? That something that leads to the death of innocent people is ineffective? Ineffective at what? Causing death? Combating crime? Who knows? Really, it just doesn't make much sense.

that you offered up a lot of reasons to like *Buffy*—even though they can't remember any of them. Add this to the fact you're cooler and more likeable than you realize, and you've just won yourself some *Buffy* fans.

All of this leads to the following conclusion: If you find yourself in a situation where you think you should say something, but are worried about saying the *right* thing, don't be. Say something. If it's genuine, and not—pardon my French—complete bullshit (more on that later), you have a real opportunity for influence, even if you feel like you're stumbling over your words. Rather than fixating on a momentary slip of the tongue or an awkward phrasing, your audience is more likely to walk away thinking about the gist of your message. More than that, they are more likely than not to go along with what you say, which is what we turn to next.

INCLINED TO AGREE

In 1975, a British philosopher of language named Paul Grice laid out his highly influential theory of conversational norms—a theory that has continued to have a lasting impact on the science of communication to this day.[18] Central to Grice's theory is the idea that communication is a *cooperative* endeavor. In order to understand one another, we must work together. And in order to do that, we must have some ground rules, which Grice called maxims. According to Grice, the very first maxim of communication is that people should only say what is true, meaning that we shouldn't say something we know to be false, and we shouldn't say something for which we don't have evidence. The thing about this maxim (and all his maxims) is that it applies to both parties. Which means that not only are both people expected to tell the truth, but they should also be able to assume the other person is telling the truth. As a result, there should be no reason *not* to accept what someone else is saying at face value.

In an era of "truthiness" and "fake news," you might think that's absurd. But let's think about this for a moment. While there are times when we may doubt the veracity of what someone says, the default assumption has to be that people are telling the truth. Otherwise, communication would be nearly impossible. If I challenged you on whether you read every book you claimed to have read, and whether the salmon you had last night was really overcooked, we'd never get anywhere. What this means is that we are inclined to believe what people tell us. Which means that other people are inclined to believe what *you* tell them—especially when you say it face-to-face—rather than challenging you on the sincerity of the opinions you claim to have and the facts you claim to know.

Even more important for our purposes is that people aren't just inclined to believe the sincerity of what you say, but they are also inclined to believe the actual things you say. This assertion goes back to a theory professed by the Enlightenment-era philosopher Baruch Spinoza in 1677.[19] According to Spinoza, in order for us to comprehend a piece of information, we must first accept it as true. Once we've done that, we can go on to dismiss anything we've decided doesn't continue to ring true. We can "unbelieve" it. But "unbelieving" something is actually quite difficult. And, as we saw earlier, people don't like to do extra cognitive work. So, we often simply default to believing what we've been told.[20]

Incredibly, modern-day researchers have found actual experimental evidence for Spinoza's theory. Daniel Gilbert, a Harvard psychologist, and his colleagues conducted a series of studies where they presented participants with propositions and asked them to indicate whether each statement was true or false.[21,22] Participants were then interrupted when some of the propositions were presented, so they couldn't fully process them. This allowed the researchers to get at people's default assumption—when in doubt, do we default to *belief* or *disbelief*? It turns out that even when participants weren't able to fully process *true* statements, they still tended to assume they were true. More than that, when they weren't able to fully process *false* statements, they also assumed they were true. Overall, participants defaulted toward belief over disbelief.

Of course, if you've ever seen an advertisement and immediately been skeptical of some ridiculous claim being made, you know this isn't always the case. We don't believe everything we hear. Indeed, for distrusted sources, which many of us might consider ads to be, people's default is to reject information before fully processing it. That's why brands have to work so hard to gain consumers' trust. And that's why liberals watching Fox News and conservatives watching MSNBC *aren't* likely to default to believing everything that is said. (Although, it's worth noting, the opposite is true when *conservatives* watch Fox News and *liberals* watch MSNBC. Again, when the source is trusted, the viewers *are* likely to default to believing whatever they hear.)

Here, as in the previous chapter, it helps to remember that you're a person, not an ad, and to return to Grice's assertion that human communication is fundamentally cooperative. When conversing with another person, the default state is to trust that the other person is telling the truth and that they have evidence for the things they say. As a result, when you, rather than someone's non-preferred cable news network, express an opinion, it's much less likely to get contentious than you might think. Sure, we can all remember instances where things didn't end in such a civil manner—and those instances may loom large—but they are the exception, not the rule. You may at times experience pushback, but it is almost certainly less—and less frequent—than you imagine.

Furthermore, that pushback is most likely to occur for issues where people already have strong counter-opinions and a store of contradictory information. Although we tend to think of prototypical examples of influence, such as arguing over politics or convincing someone to do something they don't actually want to do, we regularly express opinions and attitudes on topics about which other people don't feel strongly about and/or don't have a lot of previous knowledge—and on which our opinions are therefore likely to have an even greater impact. In fact, most of what people talk about is work, relationships, money, leisure activities, other people, and appearances[23]—not politics and social issues. Before dismissing these topics as superficial, it's important to note that conversations about work, relationships, and money do shape, confirm, and proliferate social norms about what is and isn't appropriate, and who and what we're supposed to like and dislike. That means they have the potential to shape people's broader opinions and attitudes, including those related to politics and social issues. If I'm inclined to believe you when you tell me that someone was unfairly passed over for a promotion, or that someone's behavior or dress was inappropriate, you've effectively shaped my beliefs about who is deserving and why, and what behaviors are acceptable and why. And that can ultimately have an impact on the decisions I make down the road, and even the politicians and policies I support.

We tend to think people do and believe things based on their merits—that is, by considering the facts and judging and behaving accordingly. But this is a misperception. In truth, facts are less effective at changing people's behaviors and beliefs than social norms or knowing what other people believe and are doing. It means that simply by stating what you think—by doing your part to shape what others perceive as normative or appropriate—you have a bigger impact on what other people think and do than you realize.

Before we go on, you may be wondering—is all of this a good thing? Sure, it's nice to know that your statements aren't being picked apart as much as you might think, and that people are more inclined to believe what you tell them than to reject it, but that means a lot of statements aren't being picked apart as much as they should be, and that people may, frankly, be a bit gullible. Well, yes. We'll discuss in a later chapter how processing information at the most basic "gist" level and accepting it without fully vetting it can lead to a proliferation of misinformation and other undesirable consequences.

But for now, we'll focus on the upside, which is that you can probably relax your fears about becoming the next target of the moral outrage machine. The chance of someone jumping down your throat for saying the wrong thing during a conversation is slim. In fact, people are more inclined than not to believe and accept the things you say. That is, as long as you refrain from shouting at them.

YOU NEED TO CALM DOWN

While we may hold back in some contexts for fear of saying the wrong thing, if you've ever seen someone you care about engaging in an unhealthy or reckless or otherwise self-defeating behavior, you know there are other contexts where the opposite impulse grabs hold. In such instances, it can be hard not to yell at the person to try to get them to change. Stop smoking! Start exercising! Stay in school! Just do it!

A quick glance at any social media platform suggests that concern over the well-being of our loved ones is not the only context in which we resort to shouting. When we are sure we are right, or know what's best for someone, we can be startlingly brash in stating so. However, rather than representing confidence, that brashness is likely in part to be the result of the overwhelming *underconfidence* we have in our power of persuasion. People shout when they think someone isn't listening. But, as we've seen, people are inclined to listen to and accept what we say more than we realize. Here again it turns out that people's theories about the best way to influence someone aren't quite aligned with reality.

In a series of studies, Ann Kronrod, Amir Grinstein, and Luc Wathieu examined the question of whether people overestimate how assertive they need to be in order to persuade another person.[24] In one study, they described to participants a hypothetical person named "Kate" who was experiencing some health concerns they were told could be remedied by changes in her diet. The health concerns were either serious (e.g., terrible headaches and dehydration that was said to have led to her hospitalization), indicating that she really did need some advice on how to manage her health. Or, they weren't that serious (e.g., minor headaches and some slight weakness), suggesting she wasn't in any particularly dire need of advice. In addition, participants were told that Kate either was interested in getting advice from online sources, friends, or medical professionals, or wasn't interested in getting any advice. Finally, participants were asked which of two messages they would prefer to send to Kate. One message was fairly gentle ("For your health—you could eat more vegetables every day"), while the other was more commanding ("For your health—eat more vegetables every day!").

You might think that if someone didn't want advice, but you were going to go ahead and offer some anyway, you would take the gentler approach. Well, that's not what participants did. Participants in the study paid absolutely no attention to the extent to which Kate wanted advice. They based their choice of messaging entirely on the seriousness of her described ailments, or the extent to which they felt that she needed advice. In other words, when participants heard about this person whose health was in serious need of an overhaul, who seemed to be truly suffering for reasons that seemed within her control, they chose to yell at her. And they did so with no regard as to whether or not she was open to hearing their advice.

Does this sound familiar? Perhaps you have someone in your life who complains about something relentlessly that seems entirely within their control to change. It's frustrating. Perhaps even reading about Kate being hospitalized for dehydration made you apoplectic. I mean, come on, Kate, just drink some damn water! But is that really the best way to persuade Kate to turn her health around? Probably not, according to Kronrod.

In another study, Kronrod and her colleagues emailed 200 randomly chosen college undergraduates with one of two messages intended to promote exercise. Half of the students received an assertive message, which read, "Dear student, do abdominal exercises for five minutes a day. Strengthen your core. Just Do It!" The other half received a very similar, but notably gentler message, which read, "Dear student, doing abdominal exercises for five minutes a day can strengthen your core. You can do it." A week later, these same students were sent a research survey they could complete for course credit; the survey asked them how much they had exercised over the past week, as well as how much they wanted to receive health advice, along with some information about their body composition (which served as a measure of how much each student presumably needed health advice).

It turns out, not surprisingly, that yelling at someone who clearly needs to change their health habits doesn't do much to help them change: The assertive message wasn't any more effective than the gentle message at getting people who really needed to exercise more (as determined by their physical measurements) to do so. Also, not surprisingly, people who don't want advice aren't more likely to listen to said advice when it comes in the form of a command rather than a gentle suggestion. In fact, participants who didn't want advice exercised *less* after receiving the assertive message than after receiving the gentler message— even if it was clear that they really did need to start exercising more. In essence, the assertive message backfired.

The only group that seems to have benefitted from the assertive message is the group of students who said they actually wanted to receive advice. Those participants did exercise more after receiving the assertive message than the gentler message. But, let's be honest, that's not really all that interesting. If someone is specifically asking for advice, of course they are going to find clear directives about what to do to be more helpful than hedging, uncertain advice, e.g., "Well, maybe you could do this...."

The more interesting takeaway here is that while everything I've said above may seem obvious to you right now, it all seems to go out the window when we are actually in the position of trying to persuade another person. We can all nod along to these hypothetical scenarios. But the next time you're faced with someone you care about who clearly needs to change their ways, this research suggests that you too are likely to try commanding them to do so—regardless of whether or not they are open to hearing your opinion—a strategy that is likely to backfire.[25]

These studies were focused on health, but this is an important finding to keep in mind for all contexts. When we are feeling particularly ineffective at persuading others, or when we feel like our message isn't landing, we tend to turn up the volume. We talk louder. But it is that overkill of influence that actually makes us *less* effective. In the studies described above, the gentler message was more effective at getting people who were otherwise not receptive to health advice to exercise more. On the whole, we seem to underestimate the power of more subtle influence. We don't trust in the fact that people like us and will be receptive to what we have to say *if* we don't shout at them. Thus, by underestimating our influence, we may overestimate how aggressive we need to be in order to assert it.

Here I should clarify that there are certain contexts, such as when people from systemically oppressed groups speak out about their oppression, where the suggestion to "calm down" is not only insensitive, but actively harmful. This is known as "tone policing," and it can derail important conversations about oppression by "shift[ing] the focus of the conversation from the oppression being discussed to the *way* it is being discussed," as Ijeoma Oluo writes in her book *So You Want to Talk about Race*.[26] As Oluo points out, "tone policing places prerequisites on being heard and being helped," e.g., someone might say, "I'm not going to listen to you if you're just going yell at me."

The pain and anger from systemic oppression is real and deep and it can therefore be traumatizing for oppressed groups to talk about their oppression. It is absurd to suggest that someone should do so in a calmer tone, or to expect that someone should prioritize politeness when pointing out racism or sexism.

The problem is that we too often react to opinions we simply disagree with or that make us uncomfortable *as if* we are being oppressed when in fact we just feel strongly about an issue. Or, we yell at the people we love to try to get them to change their ways out of genuine concern and frustration. In those cases, the research suggests we would fare better if we calmed down a bit.

THE TROUBLE WITH UNDERCONFIDENCE

Psychologists have been warning about the dangers of *overconfidence* for a long time now. Overconfidence can lead people to take unnecessary risks, make hasty decisions, and resort to shortcuts. As Don Moore and Paul Healy, two experts on the topic, wrote in their highly cited review of the literature, "The Trouble with Overconfidence," overconfidence has been used to explain "wars, strikes, litigation, entrepreneurial failures, and stock market bubbles."[27] And in the highly regarded book *The Psychology of Judgment and Decision Making* by Scott Plous (one of my favorite textbooks from my undergraduate days), Plous states, "No problem in judgment and decision making is more prevalent and potentially catastrophic than overconfidence."[28] Indeed, researchers think overconfidence is pretty bad.

Underconfidence, on the other hand, is thought to be rarer, and less problematic. Underconfidence makes people try harder, double-check their work, and listen to advice. Some people, known as defensive pessimists, spend their lives using chronic underconfidence as an effective motivational strategy. So, there are some clear positives, and if you were going to err in one direction or the other, I'd probably err in the direction of underconfidence.

But underconfidence is an error nonetheless. Yes, we may

work harder and be more open to other people's advice, but, by definition, being underconfident means we are working *too* hard and *over*-relying on other people's advice. Have you ever spent forever meticulously crafting, editing, and re-editing an email, only to get back a two-word reply thirty seconds after clicking send? Chalk that one up to underconfidence. It can be inefficient and self-defeating. It can also be a means of passing the buck to other people by soliciting endless advice, rather than taking responsibility for our own decisions, as we'll see in a later chapter.

In the domain of persuasion and influence, underconfidence can lead people to remain silent out of overblown fears of being disliked and saying the wrong thing. At other times, people may simultaneously be overconfident in what they believe, but under-confident in their ability to get their message across. As a result, they may be overly assertive when trying to get their message out there, disregarding decades of research on persuasion and social influence suggesting that less is often more.

While the last chapter focused on passive types of influence, there are plenty of times where we aim to influence people through more active means. When we reflect on our own abilities to do so, however, we often feel ourselves falling short—as the enduring popularity of articles and books on how to influence people can attest. As we have seen in this chapter, rather than reflecting reality, this may just reflect another cognitive bias of which we are unaware.

It's important to recalibrate. However large you think your social network is, round up. Whatever impression you think you make on other people, assume it's a little bit better. Whatever pushback you're expecting to get, assume it's a little bit less. And whatever advice you're about to give, you could probably make it a little gentler.

3

JUST BECAUSE YOU ASKED

MOST OF US hate asking for things. In her book *Reinforcements*, psychologist Heidi Grant devotes three whole chapters to explaining why asking is, in her words, "the worst."[1] I myself am well-versed in the awkwardness of asking. At the start of my research career, I spent entire days asking strangers for things. As a graduate student at Columbia, I was in charge of collecting data for a study I was conducting with Frank Flynn, now a professor of organizational behavior at Stanford. Each day, I would take the subway from Columbia on the Upper West Side of Manhattan down to New York's Penn Station. There I would begin my task of going up to strangers one by one and asking them to fill out a survey. I would make the same request over and over, my stomach in knots: "Will you fill out a questionnaire?" It was most definitely (to quote Grant) *the worst*. Penn Station will forever be associated in my mind with this torturous exercise.

However, it will also forever be associated with my discovery (both personal and scientific), along with Frank Flynn, that how we imagine someone is going to respond to a request is vastly different from how they actually tend to respond. In that moment before I would approach each new stranger, I would take a deep breath and brace myself for the worst: the impending rejection, the sigh of exasperation, the insult muttered under their breath. The thing is, more often than not, when I actually approached these people, face-to-face, they would look up at me—sometimes confused, but nearly always polite—and *agree*: "Okay, sure," they would say. They didn't yell at me. Or run away. They (usually) didn't even glare at me angrily for asking.

When the study was over, we were disappointed to find out that our original hypothesis (the details of which I no longer remember) didn't pan out. As we were mulling over the data, however, we discovered something that turned out to be much more interesting: the number of people who agreed to fill out the survey in the first place. It was amazing how many people had said "yes" to my request, and we wondered whether others would be as surprised as we were by how willing strangers were to agree. Since then I have put thousands of research participants in the same position I was in at Penn Station all those years ago, and after fifteen years of researching this topic, I am now confident that my experience was not unique.

In a typical study, I tell my laboratory participants that they will be leaving the confines of the lab and going out into the world to interact with actual strangers. They are told to ask these strangers for things—to fill out questionnaires, make charitable donations, lend their cell phones, mail letters, give intricate directions, and even count the number of beans in a jar (yes, literal bean counting). Before they leave, I ask my participants to guess how many of the strangers they approach will agree to their request. The last time I officially calculated, my participants had approached more than 14,000 people with these sorts of requests. And across all of these different kinds of requests, what I find remains remarkably consistent: Over and over, people underestimate the number of people who will say "yes." In fact, people are almost twice as likely to agree to the range of things my participants ask for in these studies as they expect, which is a huge effect.[2]

The first time Frank Flynn and I ran one of these studies, we re-created my Penn Station experience as closely as possible. We had participants approach strangers on Columbia's campus in New York City and ask them to fill out a questionnaire. Their goal was to get five people to fill out a questionnaire using the same script I had used over and over—"Will you fill out a questionnaire?"—and nothing more. When we asked participants how many people they would need to ask in order to reach their goal of getting five people to comply, they predicted they would need to ask about twenty people on average. When they returned to the lab to report back on the task, it turns out they actually only had to ask about ten people on average—half as many as they had anticipated.[3]

And when I say these participants "returned" to the lab, it would probably be more accurate to say that they *bounded* back into the lab. I watched one participant after another return utterly astounded by how much easier their task had been than they had expected, and by how much nicer people were than they had anticipated. Just like I was back in Penn Station.

At this point, we felt like we were on to something, but we didn't know how far we could push this effect. Did it have something to do with this specific request? Do people just love filling out surveys more than anyone had ever imagined? Or, would people be similarly more likely to agree to do all sorts of other tasks than we might expect? So, we brainstormed some other things our participants could ask for. In one study, we had participants go up to strangers and ask to borrow their cell phones to make a quick call. Once they got someone to agree, the participant would call us back in the lab and give us a little bit of information so we could verify that they were in fact borrowing different strangers' phones. They did this three times before returning to the lab. In that study, participants thought they would need to ask about ten people before three would agree, but they actually had to ask only about six.

In another study, we had participants ask strangers for directions—with a twist. For this study, we took advantage of the fact that the gym at Columbia is kind of hard to find. It's below ground, hidden away in the northwest corner of the main campus. So, it would be entirely believable for someone to walk right past it and not be able to find the entrance, which is the story we had participants tell. Participants were taken to a designated location on campus about three city blocks away from the gym and instructed to approach strangers one by one, telling them that they were having trouble finding the entrance to the gym. Then came the ask: "Will you take me there?" Participants asked strangers to walk them all the way to the gym to show them where the entrance was. Complying with this request would mean walking a stranger three city blocks, possibly out of one's own way. So, not surprisingly, participants in this study thought they would have to ask a lot of people—about seven—before a single person would agree to this request. But it turned out they only had to ask two—one out of every two people approached with this request agreed to it.

At this point, we were pretty convinced of the effect. We found the same thing every time we ran a study—in the lab with college students, at least. Time and again, request after request, our participants underestimated how likely other people would be to say "yes," and overestimated the likelihood of rejection. Now the question was: Would we find the same effects outside of the lab, for requests people weren't making as part of an experiment—requests they had an actual stake in?

BROTHER, CAN YOU SPARE A DIME?

Lucky for us, people make requests like this all the time as part of organized fundraising campaigns. Plenty of organizations rely on individual fundraisers asking other people for donations. We teamed up with one such organization: Team In Training, a program of the Leukemia & Lymphoma Society that raises money for clinical research, education, and patient care for various blood cancers. Team In Training volunteers participate in an endurance challenge (e.g., a marathon or triathlon) and are provided with a coach to help them train for the event in exchange for their fundraising efforts. This was a great context to test whether our effect generalized to the real world because the task these fundraisers sign up for is basically a natural replication of the kinds of studies we had already been doing in the lab. And, as a bonus, the size of the task participants are typically expected to complete is significant. At the time of our study, the minimum amount of money participants needed to raise in order to participate was between $2,100 and $5,000—a much more daunting task than getting five people to fill out a survey.

The Team In Training organizers kindly allowed us to recruit participants at their information sessions in New York City, and we got more than 100 participants to sign up for our study. These volunteers did essentially the same task as the participants in our lab studies. First, they filled out a questionnaire where they had to guess the number of people they would need to ask in order to meet their fundraising goal. Then, at the end of the fundraising period (about five months later), they reported back on how many people they actually had to ask in order to reach their goal. Luckily, we didn't have to rely solely on participants' memories during this period. Another advantage of working with Team In Training is that the organization had participants keep an accounting log of everyone they had asked for donations, so we were able to compare their memories to these logs.

What we found was remarkably similar to what we had been finding in our lab studies. At the beginning of the fundraising period, participants thought they would need to ask about 210 people on average in order to reach their fundraising goal. In fact, they only had to ask 122 people—almost 100 fewer people than they anticipated. These Team In Training volunteers, like our laboratory participants, underestimated how many people would comply with their requests—by a long shot.[4]

So, it seemed that we had stumbled upon a real finding. Our effect wasn't just a quirk of the laboratory paradigm we had been using. Even people who specifically volunteered to do an actual fundraising task overestimated how difficult that task would turn out to be.

It's worth noting that this is not a given in science. Plenty of times an initial finding turns out to have been a false alarm you find yourself chasing for years to come, to no avail. But this effect just kept showing up again and again. Not only that, the effect was *big*. I could see what was happening even before I analyzed the data—in participants' anxious expressions before they left the lab, and in their surprised, relieved faces when they returned. They couldn't believe how easy this task they had been dreading had turned out to be. It was so satisfying to see this effect over and over that my colleagues and I have continued to study it ever since—in New York,[5] California,[6] Canada,[7,8] The Netherlands,[9] and China.[10] While there are important differences in the way the effect plays out in each of these settings, the basic effect is there each time.

People anticipate more rejection than they actually end up experiencing, and getting people to comply with our requests is easier than we think. It is hard to argue with these conclusions after more than a decade of seeing the same results over and over. And yet, even people who know this to be true (such as my husband) can forget in the moment.

While I was writing this book, my husband and I were on a road trip with our two small children when we started to hear an odd sound coming from our tire. When we pulled over to inspect it, we discovered a screw embedded in the tire. We were in a small town, the weekend before the Fourth of July, with three hours left to drive and our impatient one- and five-year-olds in the backseat. We checked our phones and saw that there was a small local repair shop not too far away. But from the information online, it looked like it had just closed. We decided to drive by the shop anyway. After all, we just needed someone to pull out the screw and plug up the hole—something that should take no more than five minutes. As we pulled into the parking lot, we saw from the hours on the door that the shop had indeed closed at 2 p.m. It was 2:45 p.m. But we could see that the mechanic was still in the garage. My husband rolled down the window and asked, "You closed?" "Yup," he said. Defeated, my husband, sighed, rolled up the window, and started to drive away. "Wait!" I said. "Why don't we just tell him what we need and see if he'd be willing to help us out?"

My husband reluctantly rolled his window back down and said, "We've just got a screw in our tire, it should only take five minutes. Any chance you'd be willing to help us out?" The mechanic came out, took a look at our tire, and immediately nodded. He walked back into the garage, grabbed some tools, and said, "It's like the Hippocratic oath, I've gotta help out with things like this." He quickly removed the screw and plugged it up—it did only take five minutes. Then he sent us on our way.

What could have been an hours-long ordeal (or worse) turned into a ten-minute detour because we asked. And everyone left happy. The mechanic felt good that he was able be helpful (plus, he walked away with some extra cash as a token of our thanks—more about that later). We felt good because we got what we needed, but also because we got to enjoy that feeling of being surprised and relieved that people are more willing to agree than we think. (Even though we of all people should no longer be surprised by such things.)

There are a couple of key takeaways here that tie this experience together with the Team In Training study: First, the undue pessimism we hold about our ability to get other people to do things for us shows up when there are real stakes. Second, that pessimistic feeling is really hard to shake. My husband has heard about my studies for the entire length of our relationship, and some of those Team In Training volunteers had participated in fundraising campaigns before. But that doesn't change that fact that asking still feels like the worst, and it's hard not to let that feeling color our expectations of the whole interaction. In those moments it's worth trying to remember that you're probably better at getting people to do things for you than you realize—and you most likely don't need to bribe anyone, which is what we'll turn to next.

FOR A DOLLAR, WOULD YOU . . . ?

One consequence of underestimating the power of a simple request is that we do a lot of unnecessary things when we ask for something because we think they will increase our chances of getting a "yes"—for example, offering people money in exchange for compliance. In my telling of the punctured tire story above, I left one thing out: My husband didn't just say, "We've just got a screw in our tire, it should only take five minutes. Any chance you'd be willing to help us out?" He also added, *"We'll pay you double your normal rate."*

Many of us have this impulse to offer money in exchange for someone's compliance when we ask for something. We'll offer gas money in exchange for a ride, or beer money in exchange for helping us move. But while offering money makes us *feel* more comfortable and effective asking for something, it doesn't actually do as much as we think to increase the likelihood that you will get someone to say "yes."

In research I conducted with Daniel Newark of HEC Paris and Amy Xu, a former graduate student of mine, we compared how much higher participants thought compliance with their requests would be if they offered money versus how much money actually boosted compliance.[11] In our first study, we had participants do the same task Frank Flynn and I first used in our original studies. Participants were instructed to leave the lab, approach strangers one by one, and ask them to fill out a questionnaire until three people agreed. However, for half of our participants, we changed this procedure slightly. While half of our participants were randomly assigned to complete the task as originally designed, using the script, "Will you do me a favor? Will you fill out a questionnaire?," the other half were handed three dollars and told they would be offering a dollar to each person they approached in exchange for completing a questionnaire. They were to show each person the dollar and say, "Will you do me a favor? If I give you a dollar, will you fill out a questionnaire?" Just as in our previous studies, participants in both conditions predicted how many people they would need to approach in order to get three people to agree to complete a questionnaire, and then kept track of how many people they actually had to ask when making their requests.

Take a moment to put yourself in these participants' shoes. Imagine going up to random strangers and asking them to fill out a survey. Now imagine making this same request but sweetening the ask with some cash. Which way of asking do you think would be most effective? Intuitively, it's the ask that comes with the offer of a dollar. And, indeed, our participants overwhelmingly thought the cash would result in higher compliance. When they weren't holding dollars in their hands, participants guessed they would have to ask an average of about 10.5 people in order to get three to comply—a predicted compliance rate of about 29%. But when they had a stack of dollars to offer, they guessed they would have to ask only an average of about 6.5 people to get three to comply—a predicted compliance rate of about 46%. Amazingly, however, when we looked at the *actual* compliance rates across the two conditions, they were identical. Participants actually had to ask an average of 4.25 people in the no-money condition and an average of 4.29 people in the dollar condition. That's a difference of .04 people—completely negligible.

So, offering a dollar didn't increase compliance with this request. You might be thinking that perhaps a dollar simply wasn't a big enough incentive to increase compliance—and you might be right. However, our participants certainly thought it was big enough before they made their requests. They thought offering a dollar would cut the number of people they had to ask by 38%—quite a significant decrease in having to do something people think is *the worst*. So, why did our participants think offering money was going to have this effect?

In a series of follow-up studies designed to home in on the answer to this question, we had participants imagine themselves asking people for various things we couldn't get participants to actually ask for in our laboratory studies: to help them move, give them a ride to the airport, help them shovel snow (I live in Upstate New York—it's a thing). In one condition, we had participants imagine asking different individuals to do each of these things as favors, while in another condition we had participants imagine offering to pay people to do each of these things. Then we asked our participants a series of questions about their feelings when they imagined making these requests, and how big they thought each of these requests was.

What we found is that paying people for things does have a positive effect—on the person asking. When participants thought about offering money to people in exchange for each of these favors, they imagined feeling much more comfortable and less awkward than when they thought about asking for these things as favors. And when people felt less awkward and anxious about asking, they were able to see the things they were asking for in a clearer light.

When you are overcome with the anxiety of asking—for, say, a ride to the airport—the thing that you are asking for seems *huge*. In fact, as Frank Flynn has explained, the language we use when asking for a favor is peppered with expressions of gratitude that tend to highlight how big what we are asking for is, e.g., "I'm *so* sorry to impose"; "Thank you *so* much."[12] (This is in stark contrast to the language used by the person being asked, who is expected to graciously downplay their input, e.g., "It's no big deal"; "Don't even think about it".)[13] If this favor we're asking for looms so large in our heads, it makes sense that we would expect most people to say "no."

However, all of this changes when you add money into the mix. All of a sudden, everything becomes less emotional, less personal, less fraught. The whole exchange becomes transactional. Now I am here to offer you an exchange of money for services, and if you say "no," that doesn't reflect poorly on me; I won't feel personally rejected—it will simply mean you weren't satisfied with the exchange I've proposed. But now that I'm in this different kind of headspace, I realize that you're not all that likely to say "no," because the thing I'm asking for—a ride to the airport, or to fill out a questionnaire—isn't actually that big a deal. Now that it's my prerogative to accurately and rationally assess the value of what I'm asking, I can see what I'm asking for with clear eyes.

So, ultimately, despite the fact that small amounts of money don't make people much more likely to say "yes," they do help us to feel more comfortable asking for something, which allows us to assess more clearly what exactly it is we're asking for. And when we have that clarity of mind, we realize that what we're asking for is pretty reasonable—and therefore likely to be granted. In other words, money doesn't make us more effective at asking, it just makes us more confident.

In the story of *Dumbo*,[14] the titular flying elephant is given a "magic feather" to which he wrongly attributes his ability to fly. Despite the fact that the feather doesn't actually do anything, it gives him the confidence to fly, and he never tries to fly without it because he doesn't believe he can. We regularly offer money to people in exchange for their compliance because it gives us confidence (and because we will do anything that might help us avoid rejection). We clutch our dollar bills like Dumbo clutching his magic feather. But we don't need them. People are often just as likely—and happy—to do things for us for free.

To be clear, just because people will do things for us for free doesn't mean we should take advantage of people's time. After patching our tire, the mechanic who so kindly agreed to help us on that Fourth of July weekend tried to send us on our way with a playful "Merry Christmas!" and a wave. He clearly didn't agree to our request for help because of the monetary incentive. But when my husband shook his hand, he still handed him a bill, and told him to have a Scotch on us, not necessarily as a payment for his services—we would continue to think of this as a kindness—but as a friendly return of a favor.

As we have seen again and again throughout this book, we have more influence than we realize. And because we fail to recognize our influence, we resort to unnecessary tactics in order to wield it. We argue more assertively than is necessary, as we saw in the last chapter. And we offer money when a simple request would be just as effective, as we've seen here. Overall, we seem to discount subtler—and more effective—means of influence, in favor of assertiveness and incentives.

THE MILLION-DOLLAR QUESTION

So far, I've shown you that people are more likely than we expect to agree to relatively small requests. Even in the Team In Training study, the average donation people made in response to a fundraiser's request was $64 and the highest was around $1,000. Without doubt, those were generous donations. However, some people make legitimately huge asks that make even a $1,000 donation seem small by comparison. They ask others for millions of dollars, or a kidney, or to raise their children for them. The question is, then: Do we also tend to underestimate how likely people are to agree to these *really big* requests? Admittedly, I haven't randomly assigned my participants to ask people for millions of dollars. However, I do have data that suggests we place far too much weight on the size of a request when considering whether someone will comply.

Our intuition tends to be that the bigger the request is, the less likely people will be to agree to it. When Frank Flynn and I had some participants in our studies ask people to complete a very brief questionnaire, and other participants ask people to complete a much longer questionnaire, our participants expected compliance to be much lower for the longer questionnaire. But when they actually went out and made these requests, it turned out that actual compliance was the same, despite the difference in size between the two requests.[15]

It turns out that when our participants thought about how likely people would be to comply, they were overly focused on the costs someone would incur by agreeing to their requests—that is, the amount of time it would take them to complete the questionnaire. But people agree to requests for plenty of reasons that don't involve a calculation of the tangible costs and benefits. We just saw this earlier when it comes to offering money in exchange for compliance: Increasing the monetary benefit of complying doesn't increase compliance as much as people think it will. Similarly, increasing the size of the request doesn't *decrease* compliance as much as people think it will.

We'll go into more detail about what actually drives people to comply with requests in the next chapter, but for now, suffice to say that people agree to things for lots of reasons we tend to overlook when we're the ones asking for something. They agree because they feel guilty or uncomfortable saying "no,"[16] because they want to feel like good people, because they want to look like good people, because it pains them to see someone else suffer,[17] or out of genuine empathy and a desire to do something good.[18] Yet research shows that we tend to overlook all of these complicated reasons people might have for agreeing to someone's request, and instead assume that people agree to do things for tangible incentives,[19] and refuse to do things because of the tangible costs.[20] When we have those incorrect assumptions, we then conclude that offering money in exchange for compliance and asking for less are the ways to go.

Given all this, it makes sense that people would hold overly pessimistic views about how likely people are to comply with very large requests. After all, the bigger the ask, the bigger the tangible disincentives. But what we tend to forget is that at the same time, the bigger the ask, the bigger the need (and corresponding guilt of saying "no"), the bigger the opportunity to look and feel like a good person, and the bigger the opportunity to make a real difference—all of those reasons to say *yes* that we seem to discount. So, despite the inherent costs of agreeing to a big request, for all of these reasons, big requests can sometimes be especially hard to say "no" to.

To be sure, if all you varied was the size of a request, and you varied it by a lot—for example, let's say you went up to random strangers and asked for either $1 or $100—fewer people would agree to the larger request (to give you $100) than the smaller request (to give you $1). But the point here is that increasing (or decreasing, for that matter) the size of a request is not likely to make as big a difference as you think it will.

Not only do we underestimate how likely people are to agree to our requests, we also tend to underestimate how much effort people are willing to put into carrying out the requests they agree to. In research Frank Flynn and I conducted with Daniel Newark, we used our standard paradigm where participants go out onto campus and ask strangers for things. This time, however, we didn't just ask participants to guess the number of people who would agree, we also asked them how much effort people would put into fulfilling the request.[21] In one study, participants asked strangers to complete a series of trivia questions as part of a "scavenger hunt." Participants were asked to predict how many trivia questions people would answer. While participants predicted that the people who agreed to help them would answer an average of twenty-five trivia questions, those people actually answered an average of forty-nine questions—nearly twice as many as our participants expected. In subsequent studies, we found that people similarly underestimated how much effort other people were willing to put into writing a recommendation letter for them, taking notes for them, giving them feedback on a presentation, and explaining a new computer program to them.

We saw something similar in the Team In Training study as well. Not only did the participants in that study underestimate how many people would agree to sponsor them, they also underestimated how much each person would be willing to donate. They thought the people who agreed to donate would give approximately $48 on average, but the average donation was actually about $64—33% larger than they had expected.[22]

One reason we may be surprised by people's willingness to agree to large requests is that we tend to underestimate just how much people are willing to give to others. But more than that, as requests increase in size, the context of the request tends to change in other ways. For one, the targets of really large requests tend to be different from the targets of smaller, everyday kinds of requests. People who are being asked to donate bone marrow have typically already tested positive as a match—they've already taken steps to indicate that they might be willing to agree to such a request. Similarly, people simply aren't asked for millions of dollars out of the blue. Typically, those sorts of requests come after cultivating a relationship and learning about someone's values and priorities over a period of time. No one is going around asking random college students on campus for $1 million.

So, the question remains: Do the same sorts of conclusions we've made so far hold for legitimately huge asks? Are requesters similarly pessimistic about the likelihood that the person they've been courting all year for that big donation will ultimately agree? That's the million dollar question. . . .

CAN I HAVE A MILLION DOLLARS?

Conveniently, academia is home to a perfect sample for exploring this question: university deans. University deans are exactly the kind of group you'd want to study in order to determine whether people's expectations about how likely other people are to agree with really big requests align with reality. These are people who typically go from a long academic career involving little to no fundraising to a position in which fundraising is one of their most important roles. Suddenly, upon their appointment as dean, they find themselves in front of alumni and other donors asking for millions of dollars. And unlike people who have actively pursued careers in fundraising, newly appointed deans often aren't that comfortable with asking and don't have clear a priori expectations of what it takes to get someone to agree to donate that kind of money. That makes them the perfect sample to be able to compare relatively naïve expectations of what asking people for millions of dollars will feel like to what the actual experience ends up being like.

Take Paul Brest, a renowned former dean of Stanford Law School. According to one of Brest's colleagues, "Here's a guy who was really the epitome of an academic. . . . Yet he transformed himself into a fundraiser."[23] That transformation did not come easily to Brest. When he stepped down from the deanship he had held for twelve years, he wrote, "I vividly recall the first time I asked an alumnus for a gift: I was so nervous that I could not stop talking, and I negotiated down my initial request for $1,000 to half that amount without ever letting him say a word." According to Brest, "Fundraising was not my forte, . . . [b]ut it had to be done."[24]

Brest is now revered for his fundraising successes. A fundraising campaign he began in his deanship with an initial goal of raising $50 million was said to have "exceeded all expectations."[25] In 1999, as Brest was preparing to step down from the deanship in order to take a new position as president of the William and Flora Hewlett Foundation, the associate dean for development he had appointed to help him with this task, Susan Bell, clocked their fundraising efforts at $106 million—more than double their original goal.[26] Ultimately, according to Brest, he had surprised himself, writing, "Among the things I learned—to my surprise and to the astonishment of those who knew me before—was to be a pretty good fundraiser."[27]

As part of an ongoing research project to study "big asks," I've recently begun interviewing deans at my own university to see whether the surprise Brest conveyed about how much better he was at fundraising than he had expected is unique. So far, it seems that it isn't.

Kevin Hallock, dean of the Cornell SC Johnson College of Business, and former dean of the ILR School (my school), acknowledged that, like most deans, he was not drawn to a deanship due to a love of fundraising. But now he says it's one of his favorite parts of the job. Hallock told me a little bit about what happens when he goes into a typical fundraising meeting with a likely donor. Deans generally have a team of fundraisers working with them and cultivating relationships with potential donors. After careful consideration of a donor's interests and expected ability to give, the team will develop a number for the ask. This number can be quite high—sometimes surprisingly so—but the preparation that has gone into tailoring a request to a specific individual means that when the time comes, they are often more than happy to agree. And even when the request is higher than an individual is willing or able to give, they don't get offended by being asked for a large amount of money. Rather, they are often flattered that someone thinks they can afford that much! As in my studies in Penn Station, the worst-case scenario—the fear that someone will storm out of the room in a huff just because you asked or asked for too much—just doesn't happen.

Alex Colvin is the current dean of Cornell's ILR School. He took over the position while I was in the process of writing this book, so his recollections of his early fundraising efforts were quite fresh when I spoke to him. According to Colvin, on the day he secured his first million-dollar donation, he had gone in prepped to make an ask of $800,000. Instead, over the course of a friendly chat, the offer turned into a generous one million dollars, which Colvin graciously accepted. Like our Team In Training participants, he (and his fundraising team) had substantially underestimated the amount of money this donor was willing to give.

According to Colvin, while receiving a donation that is higher than the initial ask isn't typical, fundraising generally does tend to be easier than it looks from the outside. "People often think that fundraising is one of the hardest parts of the job of a dean," he says. However, since becoming dean, he has learned, "The secret is that 95% of the donors that you meet want to help you out. People are mostly generous and supportive of what you are trying to do."[28]

Alan Mathios, former dean of Cornell's College of Human Ecology, expressed a similar sentiment. After cultivating relationships—friendships, really—with likely donors, he thought things might get awkward when it came time for him to ask for a big donation. But in the vast majority of cases, those conversations went more smoothly than he had imagined them going, and Mathios was often pleasantly surprised by how much people were willing to give.

Of course, there are many differences between the context of asking wealthy alum to donate millions of dollars and the laboratory studies I described earlier. You simply wouldn't go up to a random stranger and ask them for a million dollars, and if you did, they obviously wouldn't agree. Context is clearly important. But despite all the differences—in the types of people involved, the situation, the motives—there remains a striking similarity: the undue pessimism about how likely people are to agree, and what they are likely to agree to. It seems that even those in positions of power, who are asking for things on a scale many of us will never even consider asking for, can still be surprised by the influence they possess and the things people will do for them. We'll return to this point in a later chapter.

YOU *CAN* SOMETIMES GET WHAT YOU WANT

Let's face it, sometimes we don't just want someone to notice or listen to us—we want them to do something for us. We want them to donate to our cause, sign our petition, or do us a favor. But that involves asking people for things, which is something we really hate.

As a result, we often talk ourselves out of asking for things that would make our lives easier, or better. We feel stupid for asking. We assume we'll be rejected. In negotiation terms, we concede before the negotiation even begins. Even at eight months pregnant, my first inclination was to stick out my belly and wait in hope that someone would offer me their seat unprompted, rather than simply asking someone for their seat. What keeps me from giving in to these impulses now is what I learned from asking all those people in Penn Station many years ago, and the experience of continuously hearing my participants express the same kind of surprise at people's willingness to comply with their requests.

When we ask for something, we tend to be overly pessimistic about the likelihood of rejection. Not only can this undue pessimism prevent us from asking for things, but it can also cause us to use unnecessary and self-defeating tactics to get people to agree to things they would have done anyway. We do things like asking for less than what we really want or offering money when we really didn't need to. Recall that Paul Brest negotiated *himself* down to half of what he originally intended to ask for the first time he solicited money from a potential donor. And my husband felt the need to offer a mechanic double payment for help he was happy to give for free. We think doing these things will boost our likelihood of getting a "yes"; but in fact, in many cases, people will do more for us than anticipated—and often without the expectation of anything in return. As we've seen, this is true for small requests, like asking a stranger on the street to fill out a survey, as well as for large requests, like asking a potential donor for a million-dollar contribution.

After years of studying the topic of asking, I now know that people are much more likely to agree to do things for us—for free—than we think. So, knowing what I know now, do I incessantly ask people for things? No. But explicitly asking for what I want now feels like a tangible option for getting it, so I no longer feel like I'm helplessly waiting for someone to step up and offer me their seat. I'm also more aware of the power of my requests, so I use them wisely—a point we'll return to in the next couple of chapters.

4

WHY IT'S SO HARD
TO SAY "NO"

WHEN I TELL participants in my studies they will be leaving the lab and asking actual living, breathing strangers for things, there is a palpable tension. Most of them immediately start dreading these interactions. But when they come back to the lab after having completed this task, they are practically joyful. The interactions they end up having are so much easier and more pleasant than they anticipated. As I said in the previous chapter, some literally bound back into the lab.

But this is where things get more complicated—and, I think, more interesting—than the simple story we've been telling so far. While my participants are high off of their success, I don't immediately tell them that the real reason so many people say "yes" is, in large part, because it's so hard to say "no." On some level, we all know this to be true, because we've all experienced how hard it is to say "no" ourselves. We end up agreeing to things—committee work, lunch dates, favors—that we wish we hadn't. But we forget this when we are the ones asking—especially when we're asking strangers. Not only does this cause us to overestimate how likely we are to be rejected, it also leads us to ask for things in less effective ways, as we will see in this chapter.

THE UNBEARABLE FEAR OF EMBARRASSMENT

Why is it so hard to say "no"? It turns out, sociologists have been talking about the answer to this question for years, but instead of calling it "influence," they call it "politeness." That's right, you just agreed to organize that annoying event out of a deep-seated allegiance to good manners. One of the biggest names in sociology, Erving Goffman, used a more technical term. He called it "facework."[1] "Face" is how you present yourself in public: the person you claim to be, and the things you presume it is reasonable to ask of another person. An expectation of civil society is that we protect other people's face, and they protect ours. So, if Sally says she regrets that she couldn't attend your event because she was terribly ill, and you say, "No you weren't! Rebecca said she saw you at the pub last night," you've failed at the task of "facework." Of course, we usually *don't* do things like this— challenge another person's "face"—because it is incredibly uncomfortable for everyone involved. Now Sally's turning red, Rebecca is slinking away, and you're not feeling so hot yourself.

When I ask you for something, the same processes are at play. If I go up to you and ask to borrow your cell phone, the subtext of this ask is that I am a trustworthy person and that asking to borrow your cell phone is a reasonable request. If you, in turn, say "no," you have just challenged me on those assumptions. Saying "no" to someone who is asking to borrow your cell phone might imply that you don't trust them to give it back. My favorite term for this phenomenon, which Sunita Sah, a professor at Cornell's business school, came up with, is "insinuation anxiety."[2] We have a lot of anxiety about insinuating something negative about someone else. So we hem and haw, and assure the person asking for our phone that any other day, really, we would love—no, we would be honored—to hand over our phone, but today we just need to make sure we have enough battery, etc., etc., to make it clear we aren't insinuating they are untrustworthy by refusing their request. But when it comes down to it, we usually don't refuse these kinds of requests, because saying "no" would simply be too awkward and embarrassing for everyone involved, and that is something we really hate.

In fact, we hate embarrassing ourselves so much, we do all sorts of things to avoid embarrassment—and at all costs. Approximately 5,000 people die from choking every year[3] in part because they stand up and leave the table[4]—rather than ask their tablemates for help—out of a fear of, you got it, embarrassment.

The late, esteemed psychologist John Sabini and his colleagues have argued that a number of the most iconic findings in social psychology can be attributed to people's overwhelming fear of embarrassment.[5] For example, take the "bystander effect," a classic finding demonstrated by the psychologists John Darley and Bibb Latané.[6] This is the finding that people are less likely to act in an emergency situation if there are other people around—particularly if there are many people around.

This effect has been demonstrated in a number of clever ways. In one memorable experiment, participants showed up to a study and were seated in a waiting room to complete some questionnaires.[7] Depending on the condition they were assigned to, they either found themselves alone in the waiting room, were seated in the room with two other participants, or were seated in the room with two research assistants who were pretending to be study participants. Suddenly, the room began to fill with smoke. What the researchers were interested in seeing was the percentage of participants who reported the smoke to someone in each of these conditions.

When participants were in the waiting room alone, a large majority—75%—reported the smoke to the experimenter. This makes sense—it wasn't just a little bit of smoke that could easily be explained away. As the researchers write, "By the end of the experimental period, vision was obscured by the amount of smoke present." So, 75% is the percentage of people in the control condition who thought the room filling with smoke was concerning enough to bring it up to the experimenter. In the other two conditions, therefore, we should assume a baseline in which approximately 75% of the participants would also feel that the smoke is alarming enough that they should report it to the experimenter.

Yet when participants were seated in the waiting room with two other participants, the percentage of times any one participant in these groups reported the smoke to the experimenter was 38%. Even worse, when participants were seated in a room with two research assistants posing as study participants who acted as if nothing was wrong, only 10% of participants reported the smoke to the experimenter. The rest of the participants "wav[ed] the fumes away from their faces . . . coughed, rubbed their eyes, and opened the window—but they did not report the smoke."[8]

This is a rather dramatic effect. Imagine these participants sitting in what by all appearances is a burning building, fanning smoke from their eyes, and trying to act calm in front of their peers. What was going on? The explanation you'll hear most often in introductory psychology courses is "diffusion of responsibility." In essence, the more people who are around in an emergency situation, the less any one person feels responsible to act. They assume someone else will, or already did, do whatever the responsible thing is to do in the situation (e.g., call 911 or report the problem to someone in charge). While this might explain why the participants who knew that others were also aware of the situation didn't feel compelled to report the smoke, it doesn't quite explain why they would sit in their seats pretending everything was normal.

An explanation that gets a little closer to illuminating this particular oddity of participants' behavior is something called "pluralistic ignorance."[9,10] Basically, everyone in situations like these feels freaked out and wonders whether something should be done. But in those initial moments of paralysis and doubt, they look around and see that no one else is doing anything. That causes them to doubt whether anything really needs to be done after all. Collectively, this results in what is often a terrible group decision to do nothing because the individuals involved fail to realize that everyone is actually thinking the same thing: that someone should probably do something—and quickly. According to this explanation, the participants in this study sat there acting normal because everyone around them was sitting there acting normal, so they assumed everything *was* normal. The idea that participants really believed choking on smoke in a waiting room was normal seems like a bit of a stretch to me. But, okay— let's investigate.

While both diffusion of responsibility and pluralistic ignorance can rationalize these participants' behavior to some extent, both of these explanations seem to fall short of convincingly identifying whatever it was that was going on inside participants' heads that was so powerful it kept them helplessly glued to their seats in the middle of an emergency. It wasn't until decades after the original studies were conducted that John Sabini and colleagues proposed their own theory of what was going on: Ultimately, whether participants were unclear about their responsibility to act, or whether they thought they were overreacting compared to everyone else, the underlying explanation for their behavior, according to these researchers, is that intervening—jumping up, tracking down the experimenter, calling 911, underscoring the urgency of the situation—had the potential to be *embarrassing*.[11] What if their interpretation of the situation was wrong? What if someone else was already taking care of things, and they would be stepping on that person's toes (and thus threatening their face)? What if they looked foolish by panicking, when everyone else appeared (on the surface) to be cool as cucumbers? Rather than confront these possible embarrassments, the overwhelming majority of participants chose to do nothing instead—to sit there coughing in the smoke, helplessly trying to play it cool.

With all of this in mind, the fact that people so often agree to our requests becomes far less surprising. Take the cell phone example again and imagine going up to a random stranger and asking to borrow their phone. Sure, if they say "yes" and hand over their phone, they might open themselves up to potential risk. What if you're a thief? What if you make an international call? What if you do something with their personal information? But, on the other hand, if they say "no," they might imply that they *think* you're a thief, or would use up their data, or would snoop around on their device. In other words, if they say "no," they risk embarrassing everyone involved. We just saw that people would rather sit in a burning building than suffer the pain of embarrassment. So, it's not much of a leap to assume someone faced with this choice would say "yes," hand over the most precious device many of us own,* and try to play it cool.

WHY IT'S EASIER TO SAY "NO" OVER EMAIL

Similar processes are at play in a series of studies you most certainly have heard of: Stanley Milgram's infamous shock experiments.[12] Typically referred to as studies of obedience and often remembered for their questionable ethics, these experiments actually have a surprising amount to say about the influence we have over others in ordinary, everyday contexts—like whether you should ask for things in person, or by email.

In these experiments, study participants were told they were taking part in a study on learning, and everyone was told they had been randomly assigned to play the role of the "teacher." The "learner"—an actor posing as a participant who was later surreptitiously replaced by a prerecorded message—was supposed to be memorizing word pairs, but he kept making mistakes. Each time he made a mistake, the participant (as the "teacher") was supposed to administer a painful shock. These shocks increased in intensity to the point where the "learner" begged the "teacher" to stop, and the learner eventually appeared to have a heart attack as a result of the shocks. The entire time, the experimenter stood behind the participant in a white lab coat saying only, "Please continue" or "The experiment must go

---

* Potentially even when there may be real hygienic concerns with doing so, e.g.: Panigrahi, Sunil Kumar, Vineet Kumar Pathak, M. Mohan Kumar, and Utsav Raj. "Covid-19 and mobile phone hygiene in healthcare settings." BMJ Global Health 5, no. 4 (2020): e002505. https://www.ncbi.nlm.nih.gov/pmc/articles/PMC7204931/.

on." The alarming statistic that is often given is that in the most famous version of this study, 65% of participants continued to administer the shocks all the way up to the highest voltage.

This study was—and is—widely interpreted as a demonstration of our mindless obedience to authority. The experimenter, dressed in his lab coat and representing the Yale University Psychology Department, exuded a certain authority, to which participants deferred. There was also an element of diffusion of responsibility. Presumably, any moral or legal blame for whatever happened would be attributed to the experimenter as much as, if not more than, the participants.

However, this is not the only variation of this study Milgram conducted. In another version, the experimenter gave orders from another room, via telephone. Strikingly, in this version of the study, only about 20% of participants gave the strongest shocks.[13] Why would being in a different room from the experimenter make such a huge difference in whether participants complied with the experimenter's requests? The experimenter was still an authority figure. He still wore a white lab coat, and the study still took place at Yale. He would still assume the bulk of responsibility for whatever happened.

This makes sense if we once again consider Sabini and colleagues' insights about embarrassment. Think of how awkward and embarrassing it would have been for participants to refuse to go along with the experimenter's request in the original study. They could have said "no"—and, indeed, if they said "no" four times, the experimenter was instructed to stop the study—but what would saying "no" have insinuated about the experimenter? That he was morally in the wrong. That what he was asking was unacceptable. That he was not who he was claiming to be (a responsible scientist). In other words, it would threaten his "face." It's "You weren't really sick, Rebecca said she saw you at the pub last night" all over again, but to a Yale psychology professor standing behind you in a white lab coat. However, when the experimenter was in some other room, and participants didn't have to turn around and look him in the face while refusing to continue in the study (and by implication call him morally corrupt), they felt much more comfortable doing so.

It's a lot easier (read: less awkward) to say "no" to someone when you don't have to do it face-to-face. This is a critical point when considering a choice we all make on a regular basis: How should I go about trying to persuade someone? Should I get them on the phone? Shoot off an email? Walk down the hall to their office? On the face of it, email can often seem like the best option. It's easy. And if we think we're likely to be rebuffed anyway, it's far less awkward to be rejected via email than in person. We may even convince ourselves that email has real persuasive advantages. After all, people can take their time to read our arguments carefully. And many of us are still (wrongly) worried about that whole "getting the wording just right" thing from Chapter 2, so email lets you meticulously craft your message. But Milgram's findings should give us pause here. Email gives the person on the receiving end an easy way out. They don't have to tell you "no" to your face. For this reason, showing up in person may in fact be one of the most effective—and possibly one of the most underutilized—influence tactics we have.

I have seen evidence of this in my research as well. Generally, when my participants approach people with a request in person, they find that people are far less likely to say "no" than they anticipate. However, when my former student, Mahdi Roghanizad, now an assistant professor at Ryerson University in Toronto, and I had participants email strangers with a request, we found the opposite pattern of results. People they emailed refused the request more often than expected. In fact, they didn't even have to refuse. They could avoid all of the pesky awkwardness of saying "no" simply by ignoring the email altogether, in ways they couldn't when an actual person was standing right in front of them asking for help. As a result, people who were approached in person to fill out a survey were thirty-four times more likely to agree than those who were asked via email.[14]

Imagine if, instead of going up to all of those people in Penn Station at the start of my research career, I had emailed them. I would have had a very different experience—and a very different take on the topic of influence!

There is, however, a postscript to this finding: Remarkably, participants in our studies had no idea what a big difference asking someone in person would make. Regardless of whether they were instructed to make their requests face-to-face or over email, participants guessed that about half of the people they asked would agree—a guess that was considerably lower than the number of people who complied face-to-face and considerably higher than the number who complied over email. Why were our participants so oblivious to what a huge difference asking in person makes? That is the question we turn to now.

WE THINK EMBARRASSMENT IS TRIVIAL

Embarrassment—and specifically, the act of avoiding it— plays a big role in all of our lives. However, we tend to discount embarrassment as a significant driver of both our own and other people's behavior. As an emotion, we think embarrassment is fairly trivial. Anger? That's probably something you should get under control. Sadness? Maybe take the day off and go cry on your couch. But, embarrassment? You should probably get over that. Can't you just laugh and move on? As we've seen, however, embarrassment isn't trivial. People make terrible decisions out of a fear of this seemingly trivial emotion, even in contexts as dire as choking, watching a room fill up with smoke, or being goaded into administering dangerous shocks to another person.

Perhaps when I described the studies above, you thought to yourself, *I* would never do that! *I* would refuse to participate in an experiment where I was asked to hurt someone else. *I* would tell someone if I saw smoke. *I* would never allow something silly like embarrassment to prevent me from doing the right thing. In fact, most of us think these things. We think we're good, responsible people; we want to be good, responsible people; and, in reality, most of us are good, responsible people. But the research shows that when confronted with these situations, most people—even if they have the best of intentions—don't refuse to participate or report the smoke when faced with the potential for embarrassment. In other words, there is a disconnect between what most people *think* they would do in these situations and what most people *actually* do in these situations—and it's the result of our inclination to underestimate the power of embarrassment. This tendency to discount people's fear of embarrassment is also one of the main contributors to the lack of awareness we have for our own influence.

To study our propensity to discount the power of embarrassment, researchers typically compare what people imagine they would do if they were to find themselves in some embarrassing situation to what they, or other people, actually end up doing in that situation. For starters, when Milgram asked people unfamiliar with the results of his shock experiments how many people they anticipated would agree to shock another participant who they could hear protesting in the other room, these third parties thought less than 1% of participants would go along with this request (a far cry from the 65% who actually complied).[15]

Psychologists Leaf Van Boven, George Loewenstein, and David Dunning tackled this question even more directly. In one study, participants were students in a large university lecture course that took place in a big auditorium with a stage at the front. As the students filtered into class, the Rick James song "Super Freak" was playing (which, I should clarify, was not what the students typically heard when walking into class).[16] They were each handed a sheet of paper with instructions printed on it. Some participants read that they had the option of dancing alone on stage in front of the class to the song "Super Freak" in exchange for money, while other participants read that *other* students in the class would have the option of dancing alone on stage for money. In this way, the thought of going up on stage and dancing in front of everyone was purely hypothetical for some participants, but it was a real possibility for others.

All participants then answered two key questions: What is the minimum amount of money *you* would be willing to dance on stage for? And what is the minimum amount of money some *other* randomly selected student would be willing to dance on stage for? When participants thought the possibility was only hypothetical, they said they would need to be paid a minimum of $21.07 on average to get up and dance on stage. However, when they faced a *real* possibility of going up on stage, they said they would need to be paid a minimum of $52.88—more than twice as much. And despite the fact that participants said *they* would need to be paid over $50 to do this, they thought *other* students would be willing to go up on stage for a measly $19.22!

The researchers called this phenomenon "the illusion of

courage," in part because it exemplifies the misconceptions we have about others' bravery. We think others are braver—less worried about embarrassing themselves in this context—than we are. But of course this isn't true. Sure, there are some people who are braver than others, but in general, we all tend to be in the same boat. You think I'd get up on stage and dance for $20, but, I'm actually saying it would take $50 or more—just like you.

Notably, this tendency to underestimate the extent to which other people are worried about feeling embarrassed is what leads us to underestimate the likelihood that others will comply with our requests—and to be surprised by how many people agree. As we saw in the previous section, saying "no" to someone standing in front of you asking for something is, frankly, embarrassing. So, to avoid feeling embarrassed, people say "yes." What the "Super Freak" study adds to this story is that when we aren't the ones faced with the immediate decision of whether to do something embarrassing, we tend not to appreciate just how hard it is for someone to overcome that fear of embarrassment. As a result, we assume that people will feel more comfortable dancing in front of us than they do. And, in the same way, we assume that people will feel more comfortable saying "no" in front of us than they do.

Not only does this "illusion of courage" lead us to wrongly assume that others would feel completely comfortable rejecting us, it also contributes to some wrong ideas we have about the best ways to ask for things. We saw earlier in this chapter that people don't realize how much more effective it is to ask for things in person than over email. But this is not the only misconception we have about the best way to ask for things.

In related work, Frank Flynn and I have found that people believe asking for something indirectly is as effective as, if not more effective than, asking for something directly.[17] In one study, which is reminiscent of the example I gave in the previous chapter of sticking out my pregnant belly in the hopes that someone would offer me a seat, we presented participants with scenarios in which they imagined asking for something indirectly or directly. In one scenario, for example, participants imagined they were standing at the top of a staircase with a baby stroller and needed help getting down. They either imagined that they caught someone's eye whom they hoped would help, or that they asked that person directly to help them down the stairs. Remarkably, our participants thought that simply catching someone's eye would be as effective as asking someone directly. But, of course, this isn't how potential helpers viewed this situation. When another set of participants took the perspective of the potential helper in this scenario, they said they would be much more likely to help if someone asked them directly. By now, this shouldn't be surprising to us, since we know that it is much more awkward to say "no" to someone who is explicitly asking for your help than to simply avoid someone's eye contact. However, it was surprising to our participants because they weren't thinking about how much more awkward it would be to avoid helping in one situation than the other. As a result, they failed to realize how much more effective it would be to ask for something directly.

Ultimately, our failure to appreciate the important role of embarrassment in driving others' behavior causes us to underestimate our ability to get others to do what we want. But more than that, it distorts our ideas regarding the most effective influence tactics. This, in turn, perpetuates our tendency to underestimate our own influence. We ask for things in less effective ways, people say "no" to us because we're asking in ways that make it easy for them to do so, and then we're left believing—once again—that we have less influence than we actually do.

WE THINK OUR PRINCIPLES WILL PREVAIL

The takeaways from the "Super Freak" study go even further. Importantly, not only does this study reveal the misconceptions we have about others' bravery, it also reveals that we think *we* would be braver if we were to encounter an embarrassing situation than we actually would be. When the thought of doing something embarrassing is purely hypothetical, we think it will be much easier—and that we'd be more likely to do it—than when it is a reality.

This is important because the question of whether we should get up and dance on stage isn't the only embarrassing question we have to answer for ourselves. We often have to make decisions about whether we should say or do something that could potentially be embarrassing in the face of things much more significant—for example, when encountering or witnessing injustice, and grappling with the decision of whether to confront it, in many cases by challenging someone's "face." Studies show that when we consider other kinds of interactions hypothetically, such as how we would react to being sexually harassed, or what we would do if we heard someone make a racist or homophobic remark, we similarly fail to fully appreciate just how uncomfortable we would feel speaking up in the moment. As a result, we think we would be bolder and more confrontational than we actually would be, and think others should have been bolder than they were.

In a study by psychologists Julie Woodzicka and Marianne LaFrance, women either imagined how they would respond if they were asked sexually inappropriate questions in a job interview, or, in another condition (which, incredibly, made it through their university ethics review), were actually asked these questions.[18] Interspersed with more traditional job interview questions, these female participants were asked by a male interviewer: Do you have a boyfriend? Do people find you desirable? Do you think it is important for women to wear bras to work?

Not surprisingly, participants in the hypothetical condition who imagined being asked these things pictured themselves confronting the inappropriateness of the questions in a number of ways: 68% said they would refuse to answer at least one of the questions; 62% said they would tell the interviewer the question was inappropriate; and 28% said they would walk out of the interview. However, of the participants who were actually subjected to these questions, not a single interviewee refused to answer even one question, and hardly any of them explicitly addressed the inappropriate nature of the questions with the interviewer.

Participants who imagined this interaction anticipated that they would feel angry, which would in turn drive them to confront the interviewer. However, participants who were *actually* asked these questions reported feeling more afraid, which led them instead to try to ignore the inappropriateness of the questions and let it all blow over. In fact, the researchers discovered that the harassed interviewees tended to have an odd response to the interviewer's increasingly uncomfortable line of questioning: they smiled. This may seem strange at first, but upon closer inspection, it turns out they smiled what are called "non-Duchenne smiles." These are smiles that don't incorporate the whole face. Although the mouth turns upwards, there is no crinkling of the eyes or movement of the cheeks, which are indicators of true positive feelings. Rather than being associated with positive feelings, non-Duchenne smiles tend to be associated with *appeasement*. So, while participants imagined that they would angrily confront someone who asked these inappropriate questions in an interview, in reality, they smiled awkwardly to appease the interviewer.

In another study by psychologists Jennifer Crosby and Johannes Wilson, participants made a similar miscalculation about how they were likely to react to an episode of discrimination.[19] In this study, a research assistant posing as a study participant mentioned during a round of introductions that he was active in the Queer Student Union, among other extracurricular activities. He then excused himself to use the bathroom, and as he left the room he bumped into the leg of another research assistant posing as a participant. On cue, the second research assistant uttered a homophobic slur. So, at this point in the experiment, the actual study participant was stuck in a room alone for one minute with another person who just said something offensive and homophobic. And unbeknownst to them, they were being videotaped.

The researchers wanted to see what participants would do during this minute, as well as what another set of participants who simply imagined this whole scenario believed they would do. When people simply imagined being in this situation, nearly half said they would confront the research assistant about the slur. However, not a single one of the people who actually experienced this situation said anything.

And if you're wondering if these same forces might also perpetuate individual racism, the answer is "Yes." We are also less likely to condemn racist remarks than we think we would be when considering a situation hypothetically. In another study, led by social psychologist Kerry Kawakami, 83% of participants who imagined a situation in which someone made a racist remark said they would reject that person by refusing to work with them on a subsequent task. However, only 37% of participants who actually witnessed someone making a racist remark in front of them refused to work with them because of it.[20] This means that while an outflowing of support may show up on social media following a highly publicized incident of police brutality or racism, it is unclear the extent to which such showings of support translate into people actually standing up against racism when it occurs right in front of them.

What all of these studies have in common is that they involve challenging or threatening someone else's "face." When a person makes an inappropriate comment, whether sexually inappropriate, homophobic, racist—you name it—they are essentially saying, "I think this is an appropriate thing for me to say." When you challenge them, you are calling them out on the "face" they are presenting to the world, and doing so would be incredibly awkward and uncomfortable. So, just like we think we would be more willing to dance on stage for money when the question is entirely hypothetical, we also think we would be more willing to act in these more consequential scenarios involving speaking up for ourselves and others in the face of discrimination. We think our anger and commitment to social justice will prevail, but our fear of embarrassment wins the day, more often than we know.

Importantly, this also means that if *you* were to unintentionally say something racist, inappropriate, or otherwise hurtful, you might not ever realize it because chances are no one would tell you. None of us are immune to saying wrong, hurtful, or insensitive things. It is inevitable that other people will at times feel angry, upset, uncomfortable, or trapped by things we say and do. Ideally, we would like to know if and when our words or actions have those effects so that we can make amends and change our behavior. However, the person who is hurt or offended may not express those feelings to us out of the paralysis that comes from their own fears of embarrassment—fears we tend to minimize, or may not even be aware of. We'll come back to that point in the next two chapters.

WHEN THE WRONG PEOPLE FIGURE THIS OUT

There are, of course, people who are acutely aware of the power of embarrassment and its role in driving behavior. One example is social engineers. These people are hackers who gain access to privileged information via social, rather than technological, means. Instead of writing sophisticated code-breaking software to figure out your password, they call you up and give you a compelling reason to *give* them your password. They harness all of the tricks of persuasion to nefarious purpose, including the awkwardness of saying "no." They say they are the new IT guy or your boss's colleague, and their victims—rather than suffer the awkwardness of challenging someone's "face"—err on the side of trust and end up handing over sensitive data.

In the book *Ghost in the Wires*, Kevin Mitnick, a former hacker who served five years in prison before reforming into a computer security consultant advising the likes of IBM and FedEx, describes how he used these tools in one notorious attack on the telecommunications company Motorola.[21] The tactics Mitnick used were both ingenious and infuriatingly simple. Mitnick would simply call up employees and chat with them, inserting carefully curated pieces of information into the conversation until his targets were convinced enough to willingly share with him their passwords, confidential corporate files, and other highly sensitive information. To be sure, some of his targets probably had their suspicions. They may have wondered if they really should be sharing information. But Mitnick knew he could count on the one thing that the research described in this chapter has demonstrated again and again: People would sooner go along with a questionable cover story or dubious request than call someone's bluff and run the risk of being wrong and embarrassing everyone involved.[22]

In one phase of his attack on Motorola, Mitnick describes calling up an employee referred to as "Steve" and making up the story that an IT error had resulted in a loss of data, which meant Steve's files would not be restored for days. When Steve predictably gets upset at this turn of events, Mitnick tells him that there is a way he could do him a favor and restore his files sooner, *if* he were willing to provide his password. At first Steve balks at this and asks Mitnick to verify his identity. But Mitnick plays along, slamming drawers and typing away on a keyboard as he pretends to be searching his own files for Steve's password, which he purportedly should have access to somewhere. Given Mitnick's commitment to this charade, it would be incredibly awkward for Steve to continue to press for his identity. It's not like he's really going to say, "You're not actually typing!" or "You're making this whole thing up!" He'd sound ridiculous and feel humiliated if he was wrong. Besides, he wants his files. So, Steve caves and offers up his password.

In another phase of the attack, Mitnick describes how he identified the administrative assistant of a project manager he had confirmed a priori was out of town (via an outgoing vacation message). Mitnick calls up the administrative assistant ("Alisa")[23] directly and says he is working with her boss, who has forgotten to send him a set of files before heading out on vacation. Alisa never challenges this cover story and indeed goes to great lengths to send Mitnick a number of sensitive files. At one point during their exchange, she has trouble sending him the files because they are being transferred to an IP address outside the Motorola campus and she keeps getting a security error. This should have been a red flag. However, instead of challenging Mitnick on the appropriateness of sending the files outside of Motorola, Alisa gets a security officer involved. Not to talk to Mitnick, mind you, but to let Alisa use *the security officer's* username and password, thereby allowing the file transfer to circumvent the security checks that are there to prevent sensitive information from making its way to people like Mitnick.

Before we write the individuals from these stories off as gullible and assure ourselves we would never do these things, let's think back for a moment to the studies described earlier. As we've seen, people believe they will be much more emboldened to say something in the face of harassment or bigotry than they actually are when they find themselves in such a situation. This situation is no different. We think we would be smarter, less gullible, and more assertive with our questioning than Steve and Alisa. But the truth is, we probably wouldn't. Our default is to trust people, not to doubt who they say they are. And if we have doubts, as Steve and Alisa might have had, we are rarely willing to raise them.

We can learn a lot of lessons from these examples. However, the one I want to emphasize here is that our oversized concern with embarrassment is a simple yet incredibly powerful mechanism of influence. The problem is that we are loath to use it this way, so it is left to the Kevin Mitnicks of the world to exploit. But it could be used for so much more.

NEVER MIND, MAYBE I DON'T WANT
TO ASK PEOPLE FOR THINGS

It should be clear by now that the fear of embarrassment is strong enough to drive people to agree to do a wide variety of things. It should also be clear that we underestimate whether others will agree to our requests because we fail to appreciate the fear of embarrassment other people have. That's why we non-hackers are so surprised by all the things people will agree to do for us.

Given all this, you may be wondering whether you want to ask people for things after all. No one wants to feel like other people are doing things for them out of obligation, because it's just too hard to say "no." And, it's true, when you ask someone for something, you are putting them on the spot to some degree. What are they going to do? Refuse and make the whole interaction super awkward? Probably not.

But here's the thing: As much as people may feel like they can't say "no," they also genuinely want to say "yes." Maybe not to giving a stranger their password, but likely to many other things you might hesitate to ask them. Sure, Alisa didn't want to be duped by Kevin Mitnick's scam, but she did want to be helpful, so much so that she was willing to circumvent security protocol to help someone out.

People want to do nice things for others. They want to feel the warm glow of helping and feel like good people. So, when you ask someone for something, you do put them on the spot, but you also give them an opportunity to feel good about themselves. Because when you leave, they won't be thinking about how obligated they felt to say "yes." They'll be thinking about what a good person they are because they helped someone out in a bind.

We have numerous psychological defense mechanisms

whose main function is to make us feel good about ourselves. We reimagine the things we've done to paint ourselves in the most positive light. We reinterpret our actions in ways that make sense and give them meaning—in many cases a meaning that emerges only after the fact.

We tend to think that what people do is the result of who they are and what they believe. For example, if you donate to charity, it's because you're a good person who believes people should donate to charity. In other words, our personal beliefs appear to drive our actions. However, psychologists have long known that people's minds don't always work like this. One psychologist in particular, Daryl Bem, proposed a theory called self-perception theory, in which he argued that the causal relationship often goes in the opposite direction.[24] First we behave, and then we use that behavior to gauge what we believe. In this way, our actions actually determine our beliefs. So, I might donate to charity for some *other* reason—perhaps someone put me on the spot by asking, and I felt like I couldn't say "no"—but, as a result, I end up believing that I'm a good person and that people should donate to charity. I didn't start out my day thinking this about charity or about myself. But once I saw myself donating to charity, I thought, "Look at me, I'm a good person who donates to charity! Donating to charity is a great thing to do!"

I'll remind you of how the participants in my studies feel every time they return to the lab after people have agreed to do things for them. They feel joyful, relieved, happy. This is not because they just convinced people to do things they really *didn't* want to do; rather, it is because other people were more than happy to be put on the spot when it meant being given the opportunity to feel helpful and effective and good about themselves.

Knowing that it's hard for people to say "no" shouldn't

discourage you from asking for help. Small favors, or even big favors, often have the upside of making others feel really good about themselves. Sure, there are some caveats. Making requests carelessly—overburdening someone, or asking for inappropriate things, as we'll discuss in the next chapter—should of course give you pause. But simply knowing why people say "yes" to our requests for help more often than we expect shouldn't deter you from asking—after all, those why questions will typically be reinterpreted in the best possible way after the fact anyway.

With all this in mind, go ahead and ask people for all the things you *should* be asking for. Ask your friends for favors. Ask your co-workers for advice. Make clear to your spouse who is on garbage duty. But, if you want these people to say "yes," remember the things we tend to do that make it all too easy for people to say "no" to us. Embrace the influence you have: ask directly, and do it in person.

5

MISINFORMATION, INAPPROPRIATE ASKS, AND ME TOO

AFTER YEARS OF watching participants in our studies ask strangers for increasingly bigger and weirder types of help and being surprised again and again at what people were willing to agree to, my students and I started to wonder just how far we could push this effect. What *else* might people be willing to agree to that would surprise our participants—and us?

It was 2011, shortly after the US subprime mortgage crisis that set off a major recession. A number of details about the housing crisis had emerged in its aftermath, and one, in particular, struck me. A critical precipitating factor to the crisis was that the credit-rating agencies, the watchdogs that are supposed to protect us from investing in shoddy stocks and securities—or at least inform us of the level of risk we're getting into—hadn't done their jobs. These agencies gave deceptively high credit ratings to what we now know were bundles of extremely risky subprime mortgages. One agency that came under fire for doing this was Moody's. At the time, Moody's was one of the oldest and most prestigious credit rating agencies out there, which made me wonder: How could this have happened? Was it incompetence? Fraud?

In an article for the *New York Times*, business journalist Gretchen Morgenson offered another explanation for how Moody's could have messed up so badly—one that sparked my curiosity and ultimately inspired one of my own favorite studies. According to Morgenson, Moody's had initially given these bundles of risky mortgages appropriately low grades. This means they were competent and did recognize the underlying risks. But then—suddenly—Moody's changed their ratings. Why?

It turns out, they changed their ratings simply because someone asked them to. After Moody's finished grading a pool of securities underwritten by Countrywide Financial, a major mortgage lender at the time, someone at Countrywide contacted Moody's to complain about the assessment. According to Morgenson, "The next day, Moody's changed its rating, even though no new and significant information had come to light."[1]

I was intrigued by this possibility. What Countrywide had purportedly asked Moody's to do was clearly unethical, and Moody's just . . . agreed? Perhaps I was naïve to have been surprised, but I was, nonetheless. And that made me think others might also be surprised by how easy it was to get people to do unethical things simply by asking. I wondered, what if instead of having participants in our studies make the kinds of innocuous requests we typically had them make, we instead had them ask people to do clearly unethical things? Would our participants underestimate how willing strangers would be to commit misdeeds when asked, just like they did when guessing whether people would agree to their requests for help?

To test this, we started small. We had participants go up to strangers and ask them to commit a white lie.[2] Our participants would go up to people and say they were supposed to be giving a marketing pitch about a new course offering, but that they really didn't want to do it. The problem, according to the cover story participants were given, was that they had to get signatures from people verifying that they had heard the pitch. Would this stranger be willing to sign their name on a form saying they had heard the pitch—even though they hadn't? Basically, would strangers lie for our participants on a signed document?

When we asked our participants whether they thought people would agree to falsify this document, they predicted that 35% of the people they approached would do so. But when they actually went out and made these requests, 68%—almost twice as many—agreed.[3] Just as participants in our previous studies had underestimated how easily they could get someone to help them, participants in this study underestimated how easily they could get someone to lie for them.

As I said, we started small. There could be many reasons why people agreed to sign that document. They may have thought it was no big deal; "no harm, no foul." They may have even reframed what they were doing as a good thing—after all, they were helping someone out of a bind. So, as a next step, we tried to come up with something our participants could ask people to do that was *clearly* wrong. What we settled on was having participants ask strangers to vandalize a library book.

Of course, we didn't want to vandalize real library books, so we made our own. We took a stack of books from my bookshelf and taped call numbers on them to make them look just like the books in the university library. We knew we had to come up with a good cover story. Participants couldn't just go up to strangers and say, "Hey, will you vandalize this for me?" We decided that participants would go up to strangers in different libraries on campus and tell them that they were playing a prank on someone. This friend they were playing a prank on, participants would say, knew their handwriting, so they needed this random stranger to write something in pen on a page of the library book they were holding.

We spent a lot of time coming up with what participants would ask others to write. Ultimately, we settled on one word: pickle. "Pickle" just sounded pranky. In the end, participants would say, "Will you just quickly write the word 'pickle' on this page of this library book?"

When we told our participants what they would be asking strangers to do, they were sure the majority of people would refuse. And judging by the things people said to our participants in response to this request, many of them would have liked to refuse. Some people hesitated. Our participants recorded a number of "Are you sure?" and "Um . . ." responses on their tally sheets. Others indicated a clear discomfort with the idea of vandalizing the book and an awareness that they were being asked to do something wrong, for example, "I'm not sure if I should . . . it's a library book?," "So, this is like vandalism?," and "I hope you don't get into shit for this!"[4]

Nonetheless, the majority of people our participants approached agreed to vandalize the book. While our participants thought just 28% of their targets would agree to write in the book, a whopping 64% actually did.[5] Even though many of those approached expressed their shock and discomfort with what they were being asked to do, most went ahead and did it— far more than participants (and I!) had expected.

Again, what we found is that people will go along with things—even things they feel uncomfortable doing—because it is even more uncomfortable to say "no." And while most of us don't go around asking people to vandalize library books—or to do blatantly unethical things—many of us have floated requests or questions that might cross the line, assuming that if someone felt uncomfortable with it they would refuse to answer the question or simply say "no." Perhaps you've asked a co-worker out on a date, assuming they would just say "no" if they weren't interested. Or, maybe you've asked a job candidate whether they were married, despite rules against asking about that kind of information, because you assumed they could choose whether or not to respond. These requests may seem innocuous at first, but they actually have serious implications for combatting sexual harassment and increasing diversity in the workplace. These are the kinds of requests we'll turn to next.

WHY MEN SHOULDN'T "JUST GO FOR IT"

2017 was a year of reckoning for many men. It was the year the Me Too movement against sexual harassment and assault, started by Tarana Burke eleven years earlier, suddenly became a household name.[6] The mind-boggling magnitude of sexual harassment and assault allegations against media mogul Harvey Weinstein came to light.[7] We learned about that creepy button former *Today* show host Matt Lauer had under his desk, which he used to lock women in his office.[8] Even the seemingly enlightened comedian Louis C.K. admitted to exposing himself and masturbating in front of aspiring mentees.[9]

In this whirlwind of accusations, admissions, and denials of behavior ranging from the deeply disturbing to the truly monstrous, there were a number of accusations and confessions that seemed more, well, ordinary.[10] Stories where the line seemed more blurred, where the behavior in question seemed less predatory, more misguided. It seemed plausible that some of these men truly didn't realize how their behavior had affected their accusers.

One especially hotly debated allegation was directed at comedian Aziz Ansari. In an article published on the website Babe, a woman using the pseudonym "Grace" detailed a date she had with Ansari, which, she said, "turned into the worst night of my life."[11] According to Grace, she started out "excited" for their date, but when they returned to Ansari's apartment after dinner, he persistently pressured her into sex, despite her expressed disinterest. Grace says she was "physically giving off cues that I wasn't interested," and later said to him, "I don't want to feel forced." But, according to Grace, while Ansari initially seemed to respond to her hesitance graciously, stating, "It's only fun if we're both having fun," he continued to pressure her throughout the night, kissing her aggressively and pushing up against her, until she left crying. Ultimately, she told Babe, "I felt violated."

For his part, Ansari released a statement in which he said that he and Grace did engage in sexual activity, but that in his mind, it was "by all indications completely consensual." He stated that he received a text from Grace indicating her discomfort the morning after their encounter, and that while everything had seemed okay to him at the time, "When I heard that it was not the case for her, I was surprised and concerned."[12] In his response to Grace's text, Ansari apologized, saying he had "misread things in the moment."[13]

Grace's accusation against Ansari blew up—not despite its perceived ordinariness, but because of it. Some people were frustrated by Grace's decision to go public with her story, dismissing the encounter as just a bad date,[14] something most women have experienced; they argued that lumping stories like Grace's together with the likes of Weinstein's offenses diluted the Me Too movement. Others thought these less egregious, but nonetheless problematic, types of sexual encounters were exactly the sort of thing the movement should be talking about precisely because they were so common.[15] The fact that Grace's experience seemed to resonate so widely provided an opportunity to talk candidly about some of the thornier aspects of everyday sexual dynamics.

The Ansari story broke only months after a remarkably similar but fictional story went viral. The story, "Cat Person,"[16] which was published in the *New Yorker*, depicts "a sexual encounter that is technically consensual, but which Margot [the main character] still considers to be 'the worst life decision she's ever made.'"[17] Of Margot's decision to sleep with the man she's gone home with, the story makes clear, "It wasn't that she was scared he would try to force her to do something against her will." However, "Insisting that they stop now, after everything she'd done to push this forward, would make her seem spoiled and capricious, as if she'd ordered something at a restaurant and then, once the food arrived, had changed her mind and sent it back."[18]

Two things became abundantly clear from the throng of reactions to both Grace's real story and this fictional story: First, women frequently agree to things—dates, even sex—they don't want to do. And, second, men are often completely oblivious to this fact.

Let's start by tackling the first question of why a woman would ever agree to go on a date, and possibly even sleep with someone, if she didn't want to. There are, of course, many reasons, but a major one is the same reason people agree to requests to hand over their phones, donate to charity, or vandalize library books more readily than we expect: They feel bad saying "no."

It may seem a stretch to suggest that someone would actually have sex with someone because they felt awkward, uncomfortable, or guilty saying "no," but as Megan Garber argues in her *Atlantic* article called "The Weaponization of Awkwardness," the same societal forces that demand women be accommodating and "capitulate to the feelings of others" can make romantic refusal feel downright perilous.[19] Sometimes it's simply "easier to get it over with than it would be to extricate yourself," wrote Ella Dawson in her blog post " 'Bad Sex,' or The Sex We Don't Want But Have Anyway," which went viral alongside "Cat Person." Dawson's post recites the questions that go through many women's heads: "Do you really want to have an awkward conversation about why you want to stop? What if it hurts his feelings? What if it ruins the relationship? What if you seem like a bitch?"[20]

Both Garber and Dawson are quick to point out that the sex that results from such capitulation—what researchers sometimes call sexual compliance[21]—is not rape. Nonetheless, each author believes these discussions are worthwhile to have in the context of Me Too because, as Garber points out, while such encounters might not be "bad in a criminal sense," they are certainly "bad in an emotional one."[22] And, as we will see later, the emotional toll alone of such encounters can be enough to have serious repercussions, such as pushing women out of traditionally male fields.

Research supports this idea that we—both men and women—regularly accept romantic advances from suitors we aren't actually interested in because we feel bad saying "no." In one study, Samantha Joel, a relationships researcher, and her colleagues asked single heterosexual participants to select their favorite dating profile from a set of profiles.[23] One group of participants was told the dating profiles were fictional, while another was told they were written by actual participants taking part in the same study. Participants were then shown a photo of the person whose profile they had chosen and asked if they would be willing to exchange contact information with this person in order to arrange a date. But there was a twist: Unbeknownst to participants, the photo had actually been preselected by the researchers to be of a clearly unattractive member of the opposite sex—someone they would presumably not want to go out with.

When participants thought the dating profiles were purely hypothetical, only 16% said they would agree. The researchers were right; overwhelmingly, participants were not interested in dating this person whose unattractive photo they had just seen. However, when they thought this was a real person taking part in the same study, 37% of participants—more than twice as many—agreed to exchange contact information with the unattractive suitor. When the researchers analyzed the reasons for this difference, they found that people were much more concerned with hurting the other person's feelings when they thought the person was real than when they thought it was a hypothetical decision.

Thus, it does seem that even if they are uninterested, people will still agree to romantic requests out of fear of hurting someone's feelings. Yet we tend not to recognize how much our concern for others is likely to factor into our romantic decisions until we find ourselves in the awkward position of actually having to reject someone.

Here it makes sense to return to the second insight to emerge from the real and fictional accounts of sexual pressure described earlier—the realization that many men seem oblivious to how hard women find it to say "no" to their romantic advances. As it turns out, this insight is also supported by research, although it's worth noting here as well that such obliviousness may not be limited only to men.

Just as people seem to struggle to recognize how hard they will find rejecting someone else, they also struggle to recognize how hard others will find rejecting *them*. In the latter case, however, rather than sparing someone's feelings we would have hypothetically bruised, this oversight may instead lead us to put someone in a more awkward position than we had intended. By "just going for it" and asking a co-worker out on a date, for example, we may not fully appreciate the uncomfortable position we may have put the other person in.

These are the dynamics my graduate student Lauren DeVincent and I observed in our study of unrequited workplace romance. We surveyed almost 1,000 science, technology, engineering, and math (STEM) graduate students and postdocs, asking them to recall a time they either pursued a colleague romantically who turned out not to be interested in them, or were pursued by a colleague they weren't interested in.[24] About a quarter of our sample reported having had at least one of these experiences. We then asked those individuals who reported being pursued by someone they weren't interested in to indicate how difficult it was for them to say "no," and how bad and uncomfortable they felt doing so. At the same time, we asked those who had pursued a colleague and were subsequently rejected what they imagined their romantic targets had felt—i.e., how difficult they imagined the other person found it to say "no," and how bad and uncomfortable this person was likely to have felt.

What we found was that suitors failed to appreciate the difficult position they put their targets in by acting on their romantic interest. Initiators of romantic advances thought their targets felt freer and more comfortable saying "no" to their unwanted advances than targets reported having felt.

More than that, people who recalled pursuing someone romantically who turned out not to be interested in them also failed to recognize how difficult it was for their targets to focus on work, and to continue to work together with their suitor, after rejecting them. While targets of unwanted overtures reported all types of avoidance and support-seeking behaviors, these same behaviors seemed to have gone unnoticed by suitors. For example, only 7% of participants who recalled pursuing someone who wasn't interested in them thought that person avoided them afterward, but more than half (52%) of participants who recalled being pursued said they tried to avoid their suitor after the fact. Similarly, only 13% of suitors thought the person they had been pursuing sought social support by talking to someone else about the situation, while 54% of the people who recalled being pursued said they did just that. And while not a single suitor thought the person they had been pursuing had considered switching careers, 6 out of our sample of 176 people who recalled being pursued by someone they weren't interested in reported that they had in fact considered switching careers as a result of the awkward position they were put in.

I noted earlier that this tendency wasn't limited to men. Indeed, it turns out that female suitors in our study also underestimated how uncomfortable their unrequited romantic advances made their targets feel. However, there is an important caveat to this finding: It was only true when we took into account whether suitors had ever been in the other person's position—that is, whether they had also been the target of an unwanted advance. People who had previously been targets of unwanted advances were more aware of the other person's feelings, even when remembering a time *they* were the ones in pursuit. The reason this matters for interpreting our gender findings is that women were much more likely to have been the targets of unwanted advances than men, a fact that has been documented many times before.[25,26] While just one in seven men said they had been the target of an unwanted advance by a colleague, one in three women said they had previously found themselves in this uncomfortable position. Therefore, women *were* more attuned to how uncomfortable their unwanted advances made their targets feel—but because of their experience, not their gender.

Hope Jahren, author of *Lab Girl*, describes in the *New York Times* the ways in which these dynamics can ultimately push women out of STEM fields.[27] Jahren chronicles a "predictable" series of events beginning with a late-night email in which a male scientist confesses his feelings to an uninterested female scientist. As the love affair taking place in his head progresses, he is entirely wrapped up in his own feelings: He "can't sleep"; he "could get fired for this." Meanwhile, she uneasily tries to ignore the notes left on her desk, and to delicately rebuff his invitations to meet outside work hours. Until, one day, she decides the easiest way out is out of science.

The world regularly tells men with crushes to "just go for it." What else is a guy, pining and tortured over a girl, supposed to do? "Just ask her out!" the exasperated friends in any buddy movie would roar. "What have you got to lose?" As I've argued elsewhere,[28] the problem with this advice is that it is based on the premise that the only person with something to lose in this scenario is the individual with the crush. Maybe it would be better for him to confess his feelings and find out she isn't interested than to go on pining. But would that be better for *her*?

Am I saying men should never ask women out who they are not 100% certain are interested in them? No. Uncertainty is part of what makes dating fun; it's where the butterflies come from. But I do think that the threshold of uncertainty at which many men feel comfortable hitting on women needs to be recalibrated. Messaging "Can I take you on a date?" to someone on Tinder is very different from messaging the same thing to someone you don't know on Twitter who primarily tweets about academic issues—an experience many of my female colleagues have had. We can all, men and women, invest more time and effort into being *more* certain that someone is interested—or is at least not completely uninterested—before confessing our feelings, or trying to get physical.

Here I'd like to note that it's heartening to see that through the efforts of the Me Too movement, many men seem to be doing just that—thinking more carefully about how their advances may have been received by those on the other side. In response to an accusation of sexual harassment against him, Richard Dreyfuss stated, "I am horrified and bewildered to discover that it wasn't consensual. I didn't get it. It makes me reassess every relationship I have ever thought was playful and mutual."[29] And in a Netflix special a year after Grace's story came out, Aziz Ansari talked about a conversation he had with a friend who said that Ansari's experience "made him think about every date I've ever been on."[30]

We all know it feels bad to be rejected. However, we tend not to fully appreciate how bad it feels to be the one doing the rejecting. As we've seen with other requests—from borrowing a phone to vandalizing a library book—it's harder for someone to say "no" to us than we realize. That means when we ask someone out on a date, or suggest they go to bed with us, we may underestimate how difficult or uncomfortable it is for that person to say "no" to us, if it turns out they aren't interested.

In a world that tells men to "just go for it," but tells women to "not make a scene," this can have important interpersonal consequences. More than that, it can impact broader societal goals related to gender equality in traditionally male-dominated fields.

IS THAT A RING ON YOUR FINGER?

I have had more conversations than I ever imagined with my female junior colleagues about whether they should wear their wedding rings to interviews. Many have been counseled or have read in some interview advice column that they should "not wear a ring or anything else that could indicate your personal situation."[31] In my experience, most of my colleagues ultimately decide not to. They don't want questions asked about their partner that could make potential employers doubt their seriousness about the position or likelihood of relocating. Clearly, your decision to divulge your personal status—as a wife, mother, or racial or sexual minority—is a deeply personal one.

It is also a highly consequential decision, as research shows that divulging such information in an interview can impact how potential employers view an applicant's seriousness about the job, willingness to work long hours, and, ultimately, their likelihood of offering them a job. In one study of academic hiring, sociologist Lauren Rivera, a professor at the Kellogg School of Management and author of *Pedigree*,[32] concluded from her field observations of hiring meetings that academic hiring committees "actively considered women's—but not men's— relationship status when selecting hires" in ways that ultimately disadvantaged women.[33] In another study by psychologists Alexander Jordan and Emily Zitek, participants who discovered that job applicants were either single or married from fictional Facebook pages rated married female applicants as less hard-working and less well-suited for a demanding job than single female applicants.[34]

I think we can agree that someone's marital status should not determine whether or not they get hired for a job. And yet, whether explicitly or implicitly, it does seem to play a role in hiring decisions. This is why we have legal protections for job candidates that allow them to keep this—and other—information private if they so choose. Questions about marital status, pregnancy, religion, and mental health, to name a few, should not be asked—not necessarily because they are illegal to ask per se, but rather because they open up the possibility that a candidate's answer to the question could be used against them in the hiring process.[35] Ultimately, it's better not to know an applicant is pregnant, for example, so there is no chance of that impacting your decision about whether to hire her.

If it's best not to know, that probably means it's best not to ask. And yet this is a place where many of us—myself included—slip up. We often forget how hard it is for people to refuse a request, or avoid answering a question, particularly when that question comes from a potential employer.

In one study of applicants to medical residency programs, researchers found that 66%—more than 7,000 out of about 11,000 survey respondents—reported having been asked a potentially illegal interview question.[36] Fifty-three percent, or more than 5,700, of interviewees reported having been asked about their marital status, and 24%, or more than 2,500 interviewees, reported being asked if they had children or were

113

planning to have children. Not surprisingly, these questions were more likely to be directed at women than men. Applicants also reported having been asked about their age, religion, and sexual orientation—all of which is protected class information, meaning that employers cannot legally use this information to make hiring decisions. And yet, as we saw above, once you have this information, it's hard not to let it color your judgment of a candidate—for better or worse.

According to the numerous interview advice articles out there targeted to interviewees, if you are a job candidate and are asked one of these questions, you should "politely decline to answer."[37] That's good advice—in theory. But at this point you probably won't be surprised to hear that the research shows it's much more difficult to decline to answer such questions than we realize. We already saw in the last chapter that women faced with an interviewer asking obviously inappropriate sexual questions felt too uncomfortable and afraid to refuse to answer. And it's just as difficult to "politely decline to answer" personally sensitive questions about whether you are married or planning to have children, but for different reasons.

But before getting into the downside, I'll start with the upside to the fact that people are more likely than we realize to answer our sensitive personal questions. As it turns out, your co-workers, neighbors, and other everyday acquaintances would be more likely than you think to answer all those questions you've been secretly pondering about their personal lives and beliefs. And, if you were to ask them those questions, they would judge you less harshly than you imagine for asking. It might even bring you closer together.

In a series of studies, a group of researchers led by Einav Hart had participants choose whether to ask other participants with whom they had no prior relationship nonsensitive questions, such as, "What are your views on pop music?" and "How many hours do you work?," or sensitive questions, such as, "What are your views on abortion?" and "How much is your salary?" Participants strongly preferred to ask the nonsensitive questions because they thought people would be highly averse to answering the sensitive questions and would judge them more harshly for asking them. However, it turns out that people were less reluctant to answer the sensitive questions than participants expected them to be, and judged participants much less harshly for choosing to ask them sensitive questions than participants had imagined.[38]

This is good news because most of us want to know more about the personal lives of our co-workers and acquaintances. And long-standing research on self-disclosure and relationship closeness suggests that asking personal questions will prompt someone else to ask personal questions in return, leading to a cycle of mutual disclosure, which ultimately brings people closer together and leads to richer, more satisfying relationships.[39]

This research seems to suggest that we should ask people *more* personal questions, not less. And, in fact, that may be true if our goal is to build a closer community with the people around us. However, when our goal is to be an objective arbiter of a consequential outcome, the takeaway is a little more complicated than that. As with so many of the findings in this book, the underestimated power we have to elicit a particular response from someone else should be used more in some contexts, but less in others.

Let's return to the context of job interviews. As a means of making small talk, many of us—particularly those of us who are put in the position of conducting a job interview with no formal human resources training—will slip up and ask about someone's kids or what their spouse does. And job candidates, more often than not, will answer these questions candidly. In part, as we just saw, this is because people are often quite happy to talk about their personal lives with others. Personal disclosure is a means of establishing rapport and closeness, and a non-negligible part of interviewing. But research shows that interviewees may also answer personal questions even when they don't feel comfortable doing so for the same reasons we've discussed previously. We are loath to offend others—particularly someone who controls an outcome as important as a potential job offer—and refusing to answer a question feels like a surefire way to insinuate an interviewer's insensitivity for asking it in the first place. It's not exactly the kind of rapport most interviewees hope to establish with an interviewer.

Thus, most people do indeed agree to answer personal questions in interviews, even if it means disclosing information about their personal lives they would otherwise like to keep private. In a study by organizational behavior researchers Catherine Shea, Sunita Sah, and Ashley Martin, they found that 83% of interviewees felt obligated to answer personal questions.[40] And although interviewers in this study were more likely to view these questions as a helpful means of getting to know a candidate, interviewees were more likely to view them as discriminatory. Ultimately, Shea and colleagues found, this has negative consequences for both interviewees *and* employers. Not surprisingly, based on the research reviewed earlier, interviewees who were asked questions about their marital and family status were less likely to be offered the job. And as for the candidates who *were* offered the job? It turns out they were less likely to take it. Similarly, in the survey of medical residency applicants described earlier, a sizable percentage of applicants who were asked this kind of personal information in an interview reported downgrading the offending program on their ranking list as a result. Therefore, it isn't just interviewees who lose out, but interviewers as well.

As Dolly Chugh points out in her book *The Person You Mean to Be*, most of us want to be good people.[41] We don't want to discriminate against job candidates, and we try to adhere to the rules that are in place to protect people from employment discrimination. But we also want to connect with people, and we know that small talk can be awkward. We may try to split the difference by asking a personal question, while assuring a candidate that they don't have to answer it. "So, do you have kids?—I'm not really supposed to ask you that, so don't feel like you have to answer." But, of course, interviewees don't really feel like they can refuse to answer those kinds of questions. So, they answer, uncomfortably. And our failure to recognize the pressure our questions put on other people to respond can have real consequences for individual candidates *and* employers, as well as for diversity and representation in the workplace more broadly.

Sometimes we make small talk in interviews or meetings by asking about people's family lives—even, as we've just seen, at times we probably shouldn't. Other times, we fill in the lulls between conversation topics and other awkward silences by "shooting the shit." Basically, we say whatever comes to mind— regardless of its veracity—simply because we feel like we have to say *something*. At the risk of overcomplicating any form of small talk whatsoever, this is probably something else we should be a bit more cautious about, a point we'll turn to next.

BULLSHIT

"Bullshitting," as defined by Princeton philosopher Harry Frankfurt, is communication without regard for the truth. It's not the same as lying, since liars actively try to discredit or distract from the truth. Rather, bullshitters have no idea whether what they are saying is true or not, nor do they care—they just say stuff.

And we all do it. According to Frankfurt, "One of the most salient features of our culture is that there is so much bullshit. Everyone knows this. Each of us contributes his share. But we tend to take the situation for granted."[42] I'll note that Frankfurt made this observation back in 1986.

We bullshit to sound smart, to fill silences, and because we think we are obligated to have an opinion on everything. To demonstrate this last point, social psychologist John Petrocelli has examined what happens when people are explicitly told that they *don't* have to have an opinion on a topic. In one study,[43] participants were told about a fictional person named Jim. Jim had been running for a seat on the city council and had a strong lead in some polls, but a month before the election, he pulled out of the race. Why, participants were asked, did they think Jim dropped out of the race?

Participants had minimal to no information about Jim. Some participants were given Jim's supposed results on a personality test, while others were provided with nothing other than the scenario you just read. With such limited information, providing an explanation for why Jim dropped out of the race would be purely speculative. Participants had no way of knowing the truth, so anything they came up with would be largely bullshit.

However, Petrocelli gave participants in one condition an

out. In this condition, participants were given the following additional instruction: "Importantly, however, you are not at all obligated to share your thoughts." Participants in the other condition were given no such caveat. Then participants in all conditions were given an opportunity to offer their opinions about why Jim dropped out of the race.

Note that *none* of the participants in this study were told that they were obligated to share their thoughts. And yet, they assumed that they were obliged to share. When the experimenter asked participants how much they had been concerned with genuine evidence and/or established knowledge when offering their explanations about Jim's decision, participants in the condition that didn't receive the additional instruction that they were not obligated to share their thoughts reported having offered substantially more thoughts with no regard for the truth than those who were told they weren't obligated to share their thoughts. Participants who weren't offered this caveat reported that 44%—almost half—of the statements they had made were bullshit, while participants who were offered this additional instruction said this of only 24% of their statements.

This is important because it suggests that our default is to say something—anything—regardless of whether we have any idea about the veracity of what we are saying. Rather than admitting that we don't know enough to have an opinion on something and staying mum, we have a tendency to blurt something out, to speculate. And as we saw in Chapter 2, something we blurt out without a second thought may in fact sound sincere to others' ears. People don't vet the things we say as much as we might think they do. They are more inclined to believe them than to disbelieve them, and "unbelieving" something is hard work. And so, bullshit, and false information, spreads.

All of this is exacerbated on social media. Online, as in "real" life, we are both consumers and propagators of bullshit. In both roles, we make mistakes that ultimately contribute to the spread of misinformation, as psychologist Gordon Pennycook and colleagues have found. As consumers of information, we are overconfident in our ability to detect bullshit when we encounter it.[44] As we have seen, our default is to believe the things we see and hear, provided they don't come from an untrusted source or blatantly challenge our pre-existing beliefs. So, while we may not believe everything we see online, on the whole we are more likely to be duped into believing false information than we are to be skeptical of true information.[45]

This is where we, as propagators of bullshit and misinformation, make our second big mistake. Even though we tend to be pretty bad at differentiating between true and false information online, we nonetheless seem to engage with the two types of information differently. As it turns out, we are substantially more likely to share, retweet, like, and thus perpetuate false information than true information. As a result, false information spreads much further and faster on social media platforms. In one study of rumors spread on Twitter between 2006 and 2017, MIT researchers Soroush Vosoughi, Deb Roy, and Sinan Aral found that certain types of false information regularly spread to between 1,000 and 100,000 people, while true information rarely reached even 1,000 people. When these researchers tracked how quickly the two types of information spread to 1,500 people, they found that false information spread six times as fast as true information.[46]

What is it about false news that causes it to spread like wildfire, particularly if people can't even tell the difference between true and false information to begin with? When these same researchers looked at the attributes of false information that seemed to contribute to its spread, they found that it was more novel and emotionally arousing, thereby eliciting more surprise, fear, and disgust than true information. In other words, the same feature that might lead a more skeptical reader to question the veracity of some piece of information—its surprise or shock factor—is the same feature that makes it so irresistible to share.

Given that there are observable differences between false and true information, it seems as if people should be able to use these as clues to judge the veracity of a given piece of information. Indeed, research shows that when people take the time to slow down and consider such information analytically, they are able to recognize false information for what it is.[47] But given the amount of information we are exposed to in just a few short minutes on social media, it's impossible for anyone to vet everything carefully.

Instead, we find ourselves retweeting, sharing, and liking information that we find particularly surprising, shocking, and emotionally arousing. And unbeknownst to us, the same information we find irresistible to share is the very information that is more likely to be false. This makes all of us responsible for the spread of misinformation to some degree. But, you may be wondering, just how responsible could I be? Who is really paying attention to my social media activity anyway? As it turns out, more people than you think.

We saw in Chapter 1 that we tend to underestimate the number of people who are paying attention to us when we're on the subway or out to lunch, akin to feeling like we are walking around in an invisibility cloak. Well, it turns out that there is an "invisible audience" we aren't aware of in our online social networks as well. In one study, researchers at Stanford teamed up with researchers at Facebook to see how Facebook users' perceptions of the size of their social media audiences compared to reality. These researchers, led by computer science professor Michael Bernstein, surveyed 589 active Facebook users and asked them how many people they thought saw their most recent post on Facebook. They then used a sample of 222,000 Facebook users to quantify the number of people who would have actually seen a given post. What they found was that Facebook users substantially underestimated the number of people who saw their posts, guessing their general audience to be just 27% of its true size.[48] While users based their guesses about audience size on their friend counts and the number of likes and comments their posts received, offering theories such as, "I figured about half of the people who see it will 'like' it, or comment on it," or, "I assume the number of people who see me are the same people who show up in my news feed," these signals are not in fact very indicative of the actual number of people who see your posts. Ultimately, participants thought their most recent post reached about twenty friends; in fact, however, the "invisible audience" of friends who would have seen the post but not engaged with it was seventy-eight—more than three times as large.

What all of this means is that when we post, share, or retweet information on social media, the audience that ultimately sees that information is far larger than we think. So, when that information is false, far more people than we realize may be misled.

Most people genuinely don't want to propagate misinformation. However, we may do so unintentionally because of the pressure to say something—anything—without regard for whether it is actually true, and because we tend to share things we read that shock and repulse us, rather than things that are more verifiable, but less rousing.

Here I want to reiterate the takeaway from Chapter 3: If you have a strong opinion on something, you should let it be known without worrying about wording it perfectly. It is still the case that people are less likely to judge you and more likely to believe you than you think. However, these same interpersonal dynamics, which can be so reassuring and empowering, can also lead to a proliferation of false information if we're not careful. So, I'll add a caveat, which is that if you don't have anything to say, it's okay to stay silent. You don't need to have an opinion on everything, and bullshitting can have an unintended impact.

THE DARK SIDE OF UNDERESTIMATING OUR INFLUENCE

This book is about underestimating our influence—for better or worse. The examples we have examined in this chapter clearly represent the "for worse" part. Just as we saw earlier that we don't realize how hard it is for others to say "no" to our requests for help, we've seen here that we may not realize how hard it is for others to say "no" to other kinds of requests we sometimes make—ones that may be or border on being insensitive, inappropriate, even unethical. And just as we saw previously how we underestimate the number of people who will listen to and believe our most impassioned arguments, we've now seen how we also underestimate the number of people who will listen to and fall for our bullshit.

While there are undoubtedly some bad actors, like Harvey Weinstein, many of us simply don't comprehend our own power over others. Because of this, we may put others in uncomfortable situations without fully realizing it. We might float an ethically questionable idea for others to consider (even just as a joke), pressure a friend to blow off work to go out drinking, or decide we should "just go for it" and ask out a co-worker who has given us no reason to think they are interested. We do these things because we assume that others will feel free to disregard, dispute, or say "no" to anything we say that makes them uncomfortable. But by this point in the book, we know that isn't true.

All of this suggests that our tendency to underestimate our influence over others has a dark side. If we don't think anyone is listening, we are likely to cast bad ideas, inappropriate requests, and bullshit out into the world, assuming (incorrectly) that people will reject our bad ideas, dismiss our inappropriate overtures, and call us on our bullshit. By placing the burden on others to tell us they feel uncomfortable or don't agree with us, we shirk our own responsibility for the things we say and the situations we find ourselves in. This has broad implications for many of our modern ills. To combat misinformation, sexual harassment, racial discrimination, organizational misconduct, and so much more, we each must recognize our own role in perpetuating or condoning these things, and take responsibility for the influence we have.

6

POWER AND PERCEIVED INFLUENCE

WHEN I WAS an undergraduate at Brown University, I had a somewhat odd summer job working as a research apprentice at a sleep lab. The principal researcher in charge of the lab, Mary Carskadon, was studying circadian rhythms—people's internal biological clocks. In particular, she was studying how our biological clocks change as we age.

As you'll see, the methods Carskadon used to study this question may seem quite strange—even masochistic. However, this research has done a lot of good. For example, Carskadon's research suggests the reason it's so hard to get your teenager to go to bed at a decent hour and get them out of bed in time for school in the morning is because there is an actual biological shift in our internal clocks that happens during puberty, making adolescents feel tired later. And this biological shift goes in direct opposition to how teenagers' worlds are typically structured—for example, with school start times as early as 7:30 a.m. Carskadon's findings have led some schools to consider reforming their start times, which may be hugely beneficial for young people's health and learning.[1]

The problem with studying circadian rhythms is there are a number of external cues, such as sunlight and mealtimes, that have an impact on people's internal biological clocks. Even just seeing the clock and noticing that it's 1 a.m. can suddenly make you feel tired. This means that, if you really want to study people's *internal* biological clocks, you must remove all of those *external* factors. Here's where my summer job got strange.

All the studies I helped to run took place in the basement of Carskadon's sleep lab. There, all the external cues that would indicate to a person what time it was—or even what day it was—had to be removed. We apprentices weren't allowed to wear watches. Or, if we had a watch, we had to turn the face of the watch inward so our participants couldn't accidentally catch a glimpse of the time. There was no sunlight. In fact, there wasn't much light of any kind. The lab lighting was kept below 20 lux (a measure of brightness), making it dark enough so that when you walked in, you had to stop and wait a couple of minutes for your eyes to adjust to be able to see.[2] And participants were given the same sorts of small meals every two hours, so they couldn't use the fact that they were, say, eating breakfast, to gauge the time of day.

At this point you may be wondering: Who were these participants who agreed to live under these circumstances for any amount of time? Well, because Carskadon was interested in the biological shift that happens during puberty, these participants were kids. Specifically, they were between the ages of ten and fifteen years old—that way, she could compare the biological clocks of kids who hadn't yet reached puberty to those who had.

These kids were technically taking part in a "Summer Sleep Camp," a two-week sleepaway camp in the basement lab. And before you think this is the worst camp you've ever heard of, the kids did do normal camp stuff. They did arts and crafts, watched movies, played games, and read books. They just did all of those things in the dark. Additionally, they all had electrodes attached to their heads, had their temperatures taken, completed reaction time tests, and spit into tubes every two hours.

As I prepared myself to supervise these young lab participants—pre- and post-pubescent kids who would be stuck in a dark basement for two weeks straight under these abnormal conditions—I steeled myself for chaos and rebellion. I thought of how we—myself and the other research apprentices, all of whom were undergraduate students—would maintain control of the lab. These kids had to do all types of annoying things over and over throughout the course of the day so that we could collect data on things such as their melatonin production and level of sleepiness. How would we get them to do these things? I imagined coaxing and arguing with them to take their tests, eat their food, and take their naps at the set times.

But as we went through our research training, Carskadon, together with the child psychologist in charge of looking out for these kids' psychological well-being, completely changed my perspective. What they said to us during our training was this: These kids will do what you tell them. They are unsure of what is expected of them, they are worried about getting in trouble if they do something wrong, and they are looking to you to tell them what to do. If something makes them uncomfortable—if you pull their hair when you're putting electrodes on their heads, if they are scared of some procedure or probe—they probably won't tell you or complain, they will just go along with it.

In other words, Carskadon and her team weren't concerned about whether we would be able to control these kids. They wanted us to be aware of the control we already had. We had to take responsibility for the power and influence we were coming into this situation with to ensure that we wouldn't abuse it, and that the kids felt comfortable with all of those annoying things we were going to be asking them to do—and which they were inevitably going to agree to.

As soon as I heard this perspective, it immediately made sense—of course these kids would be nervous and unsure, and would thus do almost anything we asked them to in this context. But then why hadn't I realized this earlier? Why had I been so focused on how to gain and maintain influence rather than on what it meant that I was already walking into this situation with a disproportionate amount of power? In this chapter, we'll turn to this question of how being in a position of power impacts people's perceptions of their own influence over others.

Power is often defined as the capacity to influence others. As such, you would think people with power—those in leadership positions, or who have substantial control over others' outcomes—would be acutely aware of their influence over others. But, in fact, power can sometimes lead people to underestimate the impact of their words and actions on others *even more*. In other words, the very people with the most influence over others may be especially oblivious to that influence. And as we will see, this bias can be particularly problematic when people in leadership positions, such as coaches, supervisors, and CEOs, stretch the boundaries of what is appropriate to ask of their subordinates.

STRIP BASKETBALL

Josh Sankes was ten pounds and twenty-three inches at birth, so large that he suffered oxygen deprivation as he was born, leaving him with a mild case of cerebral palsy.[3] Despite surgery and leg braces as a child, and ongoing tremors in his hands, Sankes grew into his eventual 7' 1", 255-pound stature and emerged as his high school's star basketball player in a suburb of Buffalo, New York. As a junior, he received a recruitment letter from Mike Krzyzewski, the famed Duke basketball coach. The following year, he received offers to play for Wake Forest, Penn State, Rutgers, and other Division I basketball teams.[4] Sankes chose Rutgers. According to John Feinstein, who wrote about Sankes in his book *The Last Amateurs: Playing for Glory and Honor in Division I College Basketball*, "He liked Coach Bob Wenzel and the idea of playing in the Big East." And, for a period of time, this seemed like a good decision.

However, two days after Sankes' freshman season at Rutgers, Coach Wenzel was fired and replaced with Coach Kevin Bannon. At first, Sankes was excited about his new coach. He knew Bannon liked him and thought they were a good match. But things soon took a turn.

Wenzel had been fired because the team had not been playing well, so Bannon was determined to turn things around. He implemented intensive conditioning and weight-training routines, and instructed his players to start taking creatine, a supplement for enhancing muscle strength. He pushed his players hard, and they did what he asked—even to the point of collapsing.[5]

One day after the team returned from winter break, Bannon decided to try something new—and well outside the norm—in order to work on his players' free-throw skills. He decided to hold a "strip free throw" contest where the players had to remove an article of clothing for each free throw they missed. Sankes, whose hand tremors are exacerbated when he gets nervous, struggled with free throws. According to Feinstein, "By the time the contest was over, Sankes and another player, Earl Johnson, along with two managers, were running wind sprints naked while the rest of the team and the coaches watched."[6]

Sankes "felt degraded and demeaned,"[7] calling the incident "the worst time in my life."[8] According to the *New York Times*, "He later developed an ulcer and became afraid of the inevitable teasing that came after the Rutgers incident was made public."[9] Along with his teammate Earl Johnson, Sankes left Rutgers as a result of this incident. Both went off to play for other Division I teams, and both ended up leading their new respective teams to the NCAA tournament.[10] After leaving Rutgers, the two players sued Bannon, along with his assistant coach at the time, for sexual harassment.[11]

The statements made by the two opposing parties throughout this widely covered public legal battle lay bare the power dynamics at play—and especially how completely oblivious someone in power can be to their impact on others.

Bannon defended the strip practice session, saying it was "intended to provide some levity and fun," and stating that "Absolutely no one was forced to remove their clothes or to run."[12] Yet by insisting that the game had been entirely voluntary, Bannon revealed just how oblivious he was to the extraordinary influence he wielded over his players. Here Bannon was, a Division I basketball coach, doling out instructions in an official Rutgers practice session to a group of players who had dreamed all their lives of playing Division I basketball. These players had already demonstrated how far they would go to follow his directives—to the point where Sankes had earlier been hospitalized for four days following the extreme workouts ordered by Bannon.[13]

When he was told that Bannon had considered the "strip poker"–type drill to be "optional," Sankes responded: "Optional? How can he say it was optional? Who would do something like that if it was optional? Your coach tells you to do something, there's nothing optional about it."[14]

It seems so clear that his players felt they had no choice in the matter. So, how is it that Bannon could have failed so miserably to realize this?

THE CHOICE IS YOURS

Being in a position of power can impact people in a number of different ways. But there are two particularly notable things power does that can make those with the upper hand especially oblivious to their influence over others. First, when we have power, we make less of an effort to take other people's perspectives. This sounds bad, but it is mostly practical. Getting inside someone else's head just isn't as important if you don't need them as much—and people with power aren't as dependent on people without power as the other way around.[15]

In a study that has since become a modern classic demonstrating this effect of power, social psychologist Adam Galinsky and colleagues randomly assigned participants to either recall and write about a personal incident in which they had power over another person (the "high-power" condition) or an incident in which someone had power over them (the "low-power" condition).[16] After recalling a personal incident from either a high- or low-power perspective, all participants were asked to do the same two tasks, under the guise that these were "coordination tasks." First, participants were asked to snap their fingers five times as quickly as possible. Then, they were asked to pick up a marker and draw an E on their foreheads. What the researchers were interested in was how participants drew their Es. Did they draw an outward-facing E, which other people could read? Or, did they draw an inward-facing E, that no one but they could read?

What they found was that people primed with *high* power drew almost three times as many inward-facing Es, which only they could read, as people primed with *low* power. In other words, recalling a time when they were in a position of power made people less likely to spontaneously consider other people's perspectives—i.e., how the E would appear to someone else.

While this study was small, which makes it less conclusive and more illustrative, this relationship between power and perspective-taking has also been shown in a number of other studies.[17] Together, these findings suggest that when we are in positions of power, we fail to consider how others are likely to see and hear the things we do and say. This is important because the very times when we are in such positions—the times when we are *least* likely to consider how others are likely to interpret our behaviors—are the very times when the things we do and say impact other people the *most*.

However, it is also worth noting that this is not always the case. The research clearly shows that feeling powerful will sometimes lead people to ignore others' perspectives. But sometimes it won't. Researchers who have struggled to understand why these effects emerge in some studies but not others have pointed to a possible moderating factor that can turn the effect off and on. What they have concluded is that for people who are already predisposed to think about others—either because of individual factors, like being more prosocially or communally oriented, or because of situational factors, such as being explicitly told about the importance of considering others' perspectives for effective leadership—power can instead make them more attuned to others' perspectives.[18] This is because people inclined to view their power through the lens of prosociality are more likely to pay attention to the responsibility that comes with having power, rather than just the opportunities power affords.[19] For the time being, we will focus on the ways in which power can make us less aware of others' perspectives, but we will return to the effect of thinking about power as responsibility at the end of this chapter.

In many cases, the first thing power does is to lead people to ignore other's perspectives. The second thing power does is reduce what psychologists call "the press of the situation," the environmental and social forces that shape many of the things we do. This means that people with power feel freer to do what *they* want, rather than what the situation calls for or what others want them to do. They feel freer to be "mavericks," readily spurning group opinions and social norms, and are less worried about how they look to others.

Galinsky and another set of colleagues have tested this using the same power manipulation described above. In one study, after recalling a time in which they either had power over someone else or someone else had power over them, participants were given a creativity task in which they were asked to imagine that they were visiting a planet very different from Earth and had discovered a creature there. Participants were asked to draw a picture of this creature, and were provided with an example of a drawing that had purportedly been done by another participant.

In the picture provided to participants, this creature had wings. What the researchers were interested in seeing was how many participants would also go on to draw creatures with wings, indicating that they had been influenced by this alleged previous participant's drawing.[20]

It turned out that when participants thought of a time when they were in a low-power role, 37% copied the features they had seen in the previous participant's drawing and drew wings on their alien. However, only 11% of participants who thought of a time they were in a high-power role drew wings on their aliens. In other words, participants who felt more powerful were less influenced by someone else's ideas.

In another study, the researchers replicated these same effects, but with a different measure. In this study, participants who recalled being in a high-power role who were asked to perform a long and boring task were more likely to admit it was long and boring—despite learning that other participants had essentially lied to the researchers and told them they enjoyed it—than those who recalled being in a low-power role. Again, participants who felt more powerful were less likely to conform to others' professed opinions about the task.

Altogether, this means that people in positions of power don't feel as obliged as the rest of us to bow down to the kinds of social pressures and concerns we've discussed in this book. For example, take the fear of embarrassment that kept participants in Darley and Latané's bystander intervention study glued to their seats as the experiment waiting room filled with smoke. People in positions of power are less likely to stress over the possibility that they will embarrass themselves by taking action in an uncertain situation. They just act. In another well-known study, participants who were primed with power were more likely to take action in order to move an annoying fan that was set up to blow on them from a close proximity during the experiment.[21] It was unclear why the fan was there, or whether they were allowed to move it. But the participants who were feeling more powerful in the moment didn't care as much. They didn't ask, or stress about whether they would be judged or get into trouble. They just moved it.

Thus, people in positions of power seem to feel freer to do what they want to do. But that's not all. As it turns out, an important consequence of feeling like you are free to do what you want is that you assume that *other* people are also free to do what they want, as researchers Yidan Yin, Krishna Savani, and Pamela Smith have found. This leads people in positions of power to view others' actions as more freely determined, and opens the door for blaming others for things that may in fact be beyond their control.

In one study, participants were asked to read a series of scenarios in which, for example, their friend was forty-five minutes late to meet them for dinner as a result of traffic, or a colleague got their portion of a group project to them late due to an emergency. Participants who read such scenarios after recalling a time they had been in a high-power role were more likely to blame the other person for their tardiness—despite the fact that the other person had provided a clear external explanation indicating that the delay was beyond their control.[22]

Together, these two aspects of power—a reduction in perspective-taking, and an increase in the tendency to view others as having the freedom to do what they want—can have the counterintuitive effect of making people in positions of power especially likely to underestimate their influence over other people.

Imagine you're in a position of power and you make what you think is a mild or off-handed suggestion to a subordinate, expecting them to push back if they disagree. However, as we saw with the case of Coach Bannon, even an offhand suggestion by someone in power can feel like a command to someone in a position of low power. Or, as put by Adam Galinsky, one of the researchers involved in the previous studies, a powerful person's whisper sounds more like a shout.[23] Your subordinate will likely think your suggestion wasn't *really* a suggestion. Yet you are likely to be oblivious to this; you're not spending time obsessing about how your subordinate interpreted your suggestion. Besides, according to your worldview, people can take or leave other people's suggestions as they see fit. That's what *you* do, after all. Ultimately, then, you may not realize how forcefully your "mild" suggestion actually came across.

One of my favorite quotes on the topic of how people in positions of power view their own influence over others is from the movie *The Devil Wears Prada*. Miranda Priestly, the Anna Wintour-esque editor-in-chief character of the fictional magazine *Runway*, encourages her assistant Andy to stab her colleague in the back by replacing her on a trip to Paris. She says: "If you don't go, I'll assume you're not serious about your future at *Runway* or any other publication. The decision is yours."[24] What I love about this quote is that last part: *The decision is yours.* Clearly the decision is not Andy's. Her boss just told her she'll have no career if she decides otherwise. Yet there is this delicious pretense that Andy somehow has the agency to refuse.

Returning to the case of Coach Bannon, it may indeed have appeared to him that anyone who felt uncomfortable with the game he had organized during his now infamous practice session could have simply refused to play. It may have seemed this way to him because he failed to consider how a lighthearted suggestion on his part likely came across to his players—as an order from their coach that they had to participate.

When we are in a position of power over someone else, we tend not to realize how little choice that person has to disagree with us or go against our suggestions. Like Miranda Priestly or Kevin Bannon, we see ourselves as making proposals that are optional, even though it doesn't at all feel that way to the other person. All of this means that people in positions of power should think twice about the things they ask others to do. As we'll turn to next, it also means that people in positions of power should think twice before sleeping with someone whom they have power over.

McLOVIN' (OR WHY BOSSES SHOULDN'T SLEEP WITH THEIR SUBORDINATES)

On October 27, 2019, Katie Hill, a Democratic congresswoman from California who had unseated a Republican incumbent less than a year earlier, stepped down from her coveted congressional seat, much to the dismay of her supporters, over a "consensual relationship with a staffer."[25] Two weeks later, Steve Easterbrook, CEO of McDonald's, was ousted by his board, leading McDonald's to lose $4 billion in stock value,[26] over a "consensual relationship with a subordinate."*[27]

These two incidents, occurring in such close succession, led many people—across generations and political affiliations—to question whether such extreme measures were warranted.

---

* It would later come out that Easterbrook had romantic liaisons with multiple McDonald's employees.

What was wrong with these relationships after all? Shouldn't two mutually consenting adults be allowed to make decisions for themselves about their own private sex lives?

In fact, the idea that bosses shouldn't be allowed to date their subordinates, and the implementation of formal policies along those lines, is relatively new. For a long time, people argued against bans on relationships between bosses and subordinates, claiming that two adults with good intentions should be trusted to manage the power dynamics in their own relationship. Any policies limiting people's freedom to do what they wanted in their own private lives were deemed paternalistic overreach.[28] Such reasoning extended to classrooms of higher education as well. My own academic institution didn't ban "consensual" relationships between faculty and students until 2018.[29]

But recently, people have begun to seriously consider how power dynamics can color "mutually consenting" adults' romantic relationships in both the workplace and the classroom. The problem with calling such relationships "consensual," and the reason I insist on putting quotes around that word in these contexts, is that no relationship can be truly consensual if one party has so much more to lose than the other by rejecting someone's initial romantic interest, rocking the boat over the course of the relationship, or ending the relationship.

Hope Jahren, the author of *Lab Girl*, who, as noted earlier, has written about these dynamics in the context of the experiences of women in STEM fields, talks about the particular difficulty of rejecting someone's romantic advances when that person continues to have control over your professional outcomes. Describing the reaction of a typical graduate student in a STEM lab to an unwanted advance by her superior, Jahren writes, "She's worried: She has to see him tomorrow. Her thesis isn't done, and she still needs his signature. What if he says no? She's scared: If she rebuffs him, will he get angry?"[30]

As we've seen, a powerful person's whisper can sound more like a shout to the person they have power over. As a result, what may be viewed by someone in a high-power role as an innocent romantic confession, "I can't stop thinking about you . . . ," or as a request, "Can I take you out for dinner . . . ?," may sound very different to the ears of their low-power target who is worried about what offending that person might do to their career prospects or other aspirations. There is an implied " . . . or else" embedded in every suggestion and invitation.

One consequence of this unstated " . . . or else" is that people may agree to sexual encounters or even enter into relationships they would rather not. We saw this in a number of high-profile Me Too cases in recent years. Brooke Nevils, whose rape claims against Matt Lauer were detailed in Ronan Farrow's book *Catch and Kill*, said that she continued to sleep with Lauer because she was scared of the control he had over her career.[31] Asia Argento, an Italian actress and director, said she felt "obliged" to comply with Harvey Weinstein's sexual advances because she feared he would ruin her career.[32]

Yet while these are the kinds of cases that come most easily to mind when we think of abuses of power in this domain, these are also the kinds of situations that are the easiest for us to reject as being fundamentally different from our own experiences. We dismiss these sorts of concerns in our own relationships because—we are quick to note—the people we have dated have entered into relationships with us enthusiastically. They may even have been the one to initiate the relationship.

But this way of thinking suggests that the beginning of a relationship is the only point at which coercion can occur.

Similar power dynamics play out over the entire course of a relationship—we are simply less attuned to them, particularly when we are the more powerful party.

In reality, even when two parties enter into a relationship with equal enthusiasm, a power imbalance changes the dynamics of the ordinary negotiations that occur within both intimate and professional relationships—especially as the lines between the two are blurred. Some "tell-all" descriptions by subordinates of what it was like to sleep with their boss include details about new requests being added to their to-do lists at work— requests like making tea or picking up dry cleaning—which would once have been outside of the scope of the job description and borderline inappropriate, but which they now feel less comfortable refusing.[33]

It can also create a situation in which both parties do not feel equally free to end the relationship if they wish, or where one party suffers vastly disproportionate consequences when the relationship does ultimately end or become public. Monica Lewinsky, who was in one of the most famously unbalanced relationships of all time when she was a twenty-two-year-old White House intern involved with the president of the United States, said the feelings were "mutual" when she began the affair.[34] However, when it became public, she was the one who suffered the brunt of the fallout. While Bill Clinton managed to hang on to the presidency, and never suffered for work afterward, Lewinsky, who went on to obtain a graduate degree from the London School of Economics, still struggled to find a job in the years that followed as a consequence of her notoriety.

Lewinsky offered an illuminating demonstration of the power dynamics at play in the fallout of that relationship during a 2019 interview on John Oliver's *Last Week Tonight*. Responding to the question of why she didn't just change her name, she aptly noted, "Nobody ever asked [Bill Clinton], did he think he should change his name?"[35]

While most office romances don't become tabloid fodder, the arc of Lewinsky's story is nonetheless familiar. The brunt of the consequences from an exposed or failed relationship with the boss have traditionally been shouldered by the lower-power individual—the person with less work experience, fewer connections and means, whose prospects may be further complicated because their professional accomplishments may be dismissed by some people as being attributable to having "slept with the boss."

This is a major reason many organizations have recently implemented the types of punitive policies that led to Steve Easterbrook's ousting and motivated Katie Hill to resign: Ensuring serious consequences for the higher power party helps to balance the scales. Absent such measures, although sometimes even in spite of them, imbalanced power dynamics have the potential to result in sexual coercion and abuses of power, and especially to leave the lower power partner worse off.

But what if everyone involved is truly acting in good faith—as I'm sure most of us would believe to be the case in our own relationships? Wouldn't an intelligent, well-intentioned boss who developed feelings for—or began a relationship with—a subordinate recognize if he or she had crossed a line?

Unfortunately, as we've seen already, people in positions of power don't tend to realize when they are abusing that power. People in such positions assume that others will simply say "no" to things they don't want to do, and may fail to recognize the coercive nature of their power in their own relationships.[36] This can embolden them to flirt with inappropriate targets and to push boundaries they probably shouldn't in both their personal and professional relationships—believing all the while that the other person has agreed to everything voluntarily. If a basketball coach can genuinely believe that his distraught players stripped down in front of their teammates voluntarily for the fun of it, you can imagine the things a boss might believe an employee he was sleeping with was doing voluntarily.

Power also exacerbates unrequited suitors' inability to recognize the awkward position into which they've put their targets. Recall the study from the last chapter in which half of the participants who thought about a time they rejected a co-worker romantically said that they subsequently avoided that person, while only 7% of participants who recalled a time they were rejected by a co-worker thought that person avoided them afterward. It's hard to imagine those two perspectives getting any further apart, but the gap gets even wider when we look at participants who recalled relationships in which there was a power imbalance. Sixty-seven percent of participants who recalled a time they rejected a senior colleague's romantic advances reported avoiding that person after the fact, but not one participant who recalled a time they had been rejected by a junior colleague recalled that person subsequently avoiding them.

Complicating matters even further, people in positions of power may be more likely to believe that their unwanted advances are actually wanted. Research suggests that people—particularly men—can sometimes misread friendliness as romantic interest. In a classic study,[37] participants observed a friendly conversation between a male and female actor through a one-way mirror. After observing this interaction, both the actors and the observers indicated the extent to which each of the actors were sexually attracted to and wanted to date their conversation partner. Both the male actors and the male observers rated the actors as more sexually attracted to and interested in dating one another than did the female actors and observers. In other words, men in this study were more likely to infer romantic interest from this friendly conversation than women. This tendency may be particularly problematic for men in positions of power, as they may be inclined to misread the deference and friendliness with which people in positions of low power tend to greet people in positions of high power as romantic interest, leading them to erroneously assume a subordinate is as interested in them as they are in her.[38]

Relationships between bosses and their subordinates often have the appearance of being consensual—even to the parties involved. However, as we have seen, people in positions of power wouldn't necessarily realize it if a relationship—or an aspect of that relationship—wasn't consensual. That ultimately leaves it up to the subordinate to recognize and highlight abuses of power if and when they occur. However, as we saw in Chapter 4, despite how emboldened someone might imagine they would feel to do so, we tend to overestimate how comfortable we would actually feel speaking up about such abuses.

In an article Monica Lewinsky wrote for *Vanity Fair* many years after the scandal, she stated, "Now, at 44, I'm beginning (*just beginning*) to consider the implications of the power differentials that were so vast between a president and a White House intern. I'm beginning to entertain the notion that in such a circumstance the idea of consent might well be rendered moot."[39] All things considered, these dynamics don't bode well for the idea of two people managing the power imbalance in their relationship for themselves, making the case for "consensual" relationships between bosses and employees gray at best.

SYSTEMIC POWER

On Memorial Day 2020, two now infamous incidents were caught on video: One involved a white woman, Amy Cooper, who took issue with a Black birder, Christian Cooper (no relation), requesting that she leash her dog in a section of New York's Central Park where leashes are mandatory. The video captures her calling 911 and making a false report that an "African American man" (a point she emphasizes repeatedly) is threatening her life.[40] The second incident involved the murder of a Black man, George Floyd, at the hands of a white police officer, Derek Chauvin, after Floyd was arrested for allegedly paying for cigarettes with a counterfeit $20 bill. The horrific video shows Chauvin kneeling on Floyd's neck for almost nine minutes while Chauvin's fellow officers look on even as Floyd tells them he can't breathe.[41]

The sad truth of the matter is that neither of these events was unique. However, the overwhelming public response to them felt different than the response to so many incidents that came before. Perhaps it was some visceral element of the videos themselves, such as the way Amy Cooper's "voice climbed to horror-movie pitch as she leveled a phony accusation"[42] or the devastating way Floyd called for his mother while lying prone and helpless. Perhaps it was the fact that the videos came to light in such close proximity, which made it impossible to ignore the connection between the regular indignities Black Americans suffer and the violence to which they are disproportionately subjected.[43] Or, maybe the fact that people were largely quarantined at home during a global pandemic meant that we couldn't look away. Whatever the reason, these events seemed to spark a racial reckoning in both the United States and abroad. In just a few weeks, hundreds of millions of dollars were donated to racial justice organizations and bail funds,[44] sales at Black-owned businesses surged,[45] books about race and white privilege dominated bestseller lists,[46] and protests raged for weeks on end across the United States and internationally.[47]

This reckoning continued on social media, as Black Americans shared en masse the variety of indignities and injustices they had been subjected to while pursuing their career aspirations, or simply as part of a typical workday. In what broadcast journalist Soledad O'Brien called "our own #MeToo movement,"[48] journalists of color shared stories of being criticized for non-objectivity for raising concerns about news coverage of Black communities, and of having profiles of Black celebrities dismissed as "off brand."[49] Authors shared their book advances under the hashtag #PublishingPaidMe, started by author L. L. McKinney,[50] which exposed wide disparities in the fees paid to Black and white authors.[51] In my own field, the hashtag #BlackintheIvory, started by communications professor Shardé Davis and PhD student Joy Melody Woods,[52] renewed conversations about the racism that takes place in the supposed liberal asylum of academia, such as the unfair workloads shouldered by Black faculty who are asked to sit on a disproportionate number of university committees, and the ways in which research dedicated to rectifying social disparities is devalued as less important than "basic research."[53]

Then there were the indignities that showed up again and again across all of these fields: being mistaken for a custodian while you are wearing business attire, security guards interrogating you for being in the office after hours, seemingly endless remarks about your hair, being counseled to soften your tone. While any one of these instances could be written off as an honest mistake, an attempt at a compliment gone wrong, or awkwardly phrased but well-intentioned advice, scrolling through thousands of such incidents made it crystal clear how demoralizing it is to face this barrage of possibly well-meant, but ultimately hurtful, comments day after day. Not only that, but also how exhausting it is to have to smile graciously and keep all of the hurt and anger inside for fear of losing your job, missing out on future opportunities, or confirming negative stereotypes.

For many white Americans, seeing all of these incidents laid out, and knowing there were so many more unspoken incidents under the surface, was eye-opening. While this fact speaks to the effectiveness of the movement, it also raises a critical question: *Why* was this so eye-opening for so many white Americans? Given the sheer scope of these stories, how could anyone really have been oblivious to what was going on? And if you were oblivious, does that mean you were part of the problem? Inevitably, many white Americans at some point wondered: Does someone have a story about me? Would I know it if they did?

Earlier in this chapter, I said that simply as a practicality, people in positions of power make less of an effort to take other people's perspectives. Recall that the basic idea is that if I am not dependent on you for access to valued resources, I really don't need to put in the hard work of figuring out what you are thinking and feeling, your preferences and pet peeves. When I made this point earlier, you may have imagined the sorts of power dynamics we've examined so far—the relational power that exists between two individuals, such as the case of a boss and a subordinate, or of a coach and a player. However, there are other forms of power, one of which is systemic power. And one of the most entrenched examples of systemic power in American society is that of systemic racism.

Systemic racism refers to the racial disparities that are

baked into our structures and institutions. Ever since the concept of race was invented several hundred years ago as a means of justifying slavery and, in so doing, establishing a social hierarchy with white people at the top, the structures and institutions of Western, and particularly American, society have in large part served to maintain this hierarchy.[54],[55] The enduring effects of systemic racism can be seen today in the disparate outcomes between Black and white communities on numerous indicators, from the wage gap and differences in employment rates[56] to disparities in health outcomes[57] to disproportionate rates of incarceration[58] and police use of force[59] to persistently segregated school systems.[60]

This racial hierarchy has meant several things for white people. First, it has meant that white people are often the gatekeepers of valued resources, holding leadership and administrative positions tasked with deciding the fate of Black applicants to universities,[61] jobs,[62] and everything in between (e.g., awards, apprenticeships, promotions). Second, it has meant that to be white is to be the norm, the default, the non-race. As Gregory Smithsimon, a sociologist at Brooklyn College at the City University of New York, wrote in an essay in the digital magazine *Aeon*, "The most powerful racial category is invisible: whiteness. The benefit of being in power is that whites can imagine that they are the norm and that only *other* people have race."[63] This is why some Black scholars, such as historian Nell Painter, author of *The History of White People*, have called for the capitalization of *White* as a means of racializing white* people and thereby reject-

---

* Despite this, many style guides still prefer to use a lowercase w. This preference is driven in part by concerns over inadvertently legitimizing white supremacist groups who have traditionally capitalized the W in white.

ing the "comfort of this racial invisibility."[64] Third, it has meant that white people have the privilege of avoiding the uncomfortable topic of race by professing not to see race at all—a privilege people of color do not have. As Jennifer Eberhardt, a psychologist at Stanford, wrote in her book *Biased: Uncovering the Hidden Prejudice That Shapes What We See, Think, and Do*, "the colorblind message is so esteemed in American society that even our children pick up the idea that noticing skin color is rude."[65] Yet, in reality, practicing "colorblindness" is not only unrealistic, but it also reinforces the dominance of the majority by downplaying the reality of persistent racial disparities.[66]

All of this means that while Black people "whiten" their resumes,[67] engage in "code-switching" at work to look and sound more "professional" (i.e., white),[68] and generally learn to "navigate the white space as a condition of their existence,"[69] white people can pretend race doesn't exist and "avoid black space"[70] without consequence. This gives white people little incentive to seek out information about the day-to-day experiences of Black people or to proactively challenge their own stereotypic ideas.[71]

To answer the question posed earlier, this is why it was so eye-opening for many white professionals to read about the experiences of their Black colleagues on social media and elsewhere. White people have the luxury of avoiding seeing things in racial terms. Yet, as Shannon Sullivan, philosophy professor at University of North Carolina and author of *Good White People*, points out on Scene on Radio's *Seeing White* podcast, "If you can't see race, then how in the heck are you going to see racism?"[72] This means that for white people, a simple question about someone's hairstyle can be seen as just that; they may not see any inherent racism embedded in such a question. However, for someone who gets asked such questions all the time, it becomes yet another reminder that you are different, that you don't belong in this space. It is structural racism at work—an indicator of how racially segregated our world is that a fellow American's hair can seem so "exotic." For many white people, it took seeing thousands of eerily similar incidents described in one place to start to recognize the pattern, rather than viewing these incidents as individual "mistakes" or "misunderstandings."

In line with the thesis of this book, these same factors can lead white people to overlook the ways in which our *own* (speaking from the perspective of a white woman) words and actions impact our Black friends and colleagues, and ultimately serve to perpetuate racial disparities. In an essay entitled "Reflections from a Token Black Friend" that went viral in the wake of George Floyd's killing, Ramesh Nagarajah, a graduate of the US Naval Academy, wrote, "Many of the white people I know have no concept of the role they've played, passively or actively, in perpetuating these conditions." Referencing "instances most white people will recognize," such as being dubbed "the whitest black kid I know," or being criticized for code-switching, or using slang around his Black friends, he writes, "they probably never knew how damaging their words were."[73]

Chana Joffe-Walt, producer of the podcast *Nice White Parents*, makes a similar point about white people's obliviousness to the impact of their actions on people of color in a different context—public education. Wrapping up the first episode of that podcast, she evokes a very Mr. Magoo–like image: "It happens again and again—white parents, wielding their power without even noticing. Like a guy wandering through a crowded store with a huge backpack, knocking things over every time he turns."[74]

All of this means that if we return to two more questions

posed earlier, "Does someone have a story about me? Would I know it if they did?," the answers for most white people are "Most likely, yes" and "Quite possibly, no." As Naomi Tweyo Nkinsi, an MD/MPH student at the University of Washington School of Medicine, tweeted in a thread specific to academia, but which could just as easily be applied to any profession, "To white/non-BIPOC folks in academia asking yourself if you ever contributed to the things being discussed in #BlackintheIvory, let me assure you that the answer is yes. It was probably just something so inconsequential to you that you don't even remember it. . . . Understand that what was a small misstep for you could have been another painful wound for someone who has already faced a lifetime of others' missteps. I've had passive comments made to/about me that still ring around in my head."[75]

Ultimately, careless and racially insensitive remarks—sometimes referred to as microaggressions[76]—are yet another manifestation of people in positions of power being particularly oblivious to the influence of their words and actions on others. In this case, it's not necessarily the power that comes from being someone's boss or coach, but the power that comes from being the beneficiaries of an entrenched social hierarchy. No matter how well-intentioned, the "honest mistakes" of white people in this position add up, wearing on Black people, and causing disproportionate amounts of stress and anxiety at work[77] and school.[78] The consequences of this constant stress have even been observed at the cellular level in a phenomenon known as "weathering," whereby Black Americans' cells have been found to show signs of premature aging.[79] And if you have been making efforts to diversify your workplace, these sorts of mistakes can unknowingly contribute to a non-inclusive organizational culture, counteracting your own efforts by pushing your "diverse" hires right back out the door.[80]

Altogether, this phenomenon offers yet another reason why it is so critical to illuminate the lack of awareness people in all sorts of positions of power have of how our words and actions impact others. The ways in which white people can do this is by gaining perspective through paying attention to Black voices on social media; by reading Black memoirs, history books, and literature; and by, as the urgent refrain goes, listening to Black people. While we could simply try more often to take the perspectives of people who identify with different racial and other categories than ourselves, trying to do so can sometimes serve to reinforce stereotypes, as we base our ideas about what someone else must be thinking or feeling on our own preconceived ideas.[81] In contrast, *getting* perspective by being exposed to others' stories in their own words may help us to understand how our words and actions come across within the broader context of someone else's life experiences.[82] In the next chapter, we will return to this point about how getting, rather than taking, perspective is a more effective strategy to counteract our lack of awareness of the influence we have on others.

POWER AS RESPONSIBILITY

It should be clear by now that power can exacerbate our tendency to underestimate our influence over others. It is particularly difficult to say "no" to someone who has power over you, but having power makes saying "no" look easy. This can ultimately make people in positions of power oblivious to lines they may unwittingly cross.

Yet as I mentioned earlier, this effect of power is not

inevitable. Indeed, we can probably all think of leaders who eschewed this trend. People in positions of power who seemed acutely aware of the impact of their words, actions, and decisions on other people. Some leaders, aware of how compelled subordinates might feel to conform to their opinions, make a conscious effort to speak last, as President Obama has been said to have done.[83] Others cultivate a culture of helping in which senior executives don't need to be asked to jump in and offer an assist on a project, like the culture created by David Kelley at IDEO.[84] Still others have the insight to look around and recognize the impact of their mere presence, even when they may not like what they see. For example, Alexis Ohanian, co-founder of the social news website Reddit, decided to step down from the company's board out of the recognition that, as a white man occupying that seat, his presence was one more barrier to increasing diversity at the company.[85] All of this can be summed up by a line President-Elect John F. Kennedy chose to represent his newfound "responsibilities to the state" in a speech following his election: "For those whom much is given, much is required."[86]

Why does power lead some people to become less aware of their influence over others, while others seem to become more aware—at times even feeling burdened by the weight of their influence? The difference seems to be in the way someone construes their power over others. Do they think about the fact that they are in control of other people's outcomes, or the fact that they are *responsible* for other people's outcomes?

All power comes with both opportunity and responsibility. A fund manager who controls a client's investments has both the opportunity to enrich themselves and the responsibility to secure their client's retirement. A CEO of a company has both the opportunity to come up with their own vision for the company and the responsibility to employees and shareholders to ensure that direction is successful.

Yet while power inherently comes with both of these attributes, most people, particularly in Western cultures, tend to be more attuned to the opportunities afforded by power than the responsibilities that come along with it.[87] We want to be the team leader because of the career opportunities it will open up for us, yet we give less consideration to the responsibility we will shoulder for the team's performance if we are given that role.

Research even finds that when people are reminded of the responsibility that comes with power, the prospect of having power becomes much less appealing. In one study led by psychologist Annika Scholl, participants who were made team captain, and were then reminded of their eventual responsibility to determine how a bonus would be distributed among team members, experienced a cardiovascular stress response.[88] In another study by psychologist Kai Sassenberg and colleagues, participants who were prompted to think about the responsibilities associated with having power reported being less interested in joining a high-power group.[89]

Yet, regardless of how atypical and stressful it is for many of us to focus on the responsibilities that come with having power, there are people in positions of power who do construe their power primarily in terms of responsibility. These are the people who are more likely to recognize the influence they wield with their power—and to be mindful of how they use that influence.

This is because people who construe power as responsibility tend to focus more on others than themselves. If I am thinking about the responsibility I have for people who are dependent on me, I am focused on their potential outcomes, thoughts, and feelings—not only my own. That means that when I have an impulse or make a decision, I am likely to think carefully about how following through on that impulse or making that decision will impact others. I'm likely to think about the awkward position I would put my employee in by asking her out, or how hard it would be for one of my players to tell me I had pushed him too far during a drill.

As a result, research finds that people who think of their power in terms of responsibility assign fairer workloads[90] and show greater interpersonal sensitivity.[91] They may also be less cavalier about crossing lines and making the kinds of inappropriate requests we saw earlier in this chapter.

Josh Sankes, the basketball player we met earlier in this chapter, was lucky enough to finish out his athletic career playing under a coach who clearly thought about his role in this way. Following the strip basketball incident at Rutgers, Sankes transferred to Holy Cross, where Ralph Willard was head basketball coach. A highly respected coach, Willard has equated success in coaching to being "attuned to people's feelings."[92]

Rather than dismissing the Rutgers incident as just fun and games, Willard acknowledged its devastating impact on Sankes, and the "heart and courage" it had taken for Sankes to move forward. After a difficult first year, during which Sankes questioned whether he even wanted to continue playing basketball, Willard eventually helped Sankes rebuild his confidence, and, as a result, Sankes ended up leading Holy Cross to the NCAA tournament. According to Willard, "The biggest thing was to get him to trust me and to let him know that I cared about him as a person."[93]

Leaders like Willard are a reminder that it is not inevitable that power will make a person oblivious to their influence over others. There are ways in which you can have power *and* still think about others. But to do so, you must be reoriented toward the part of power that people aren't typically attuned to—the responsibility that comes with it, which brings into focus the impact you have on others.

People in positions of power have a disproportionate amount of influence over others. At the same time, the psychological experience of having power can make it even harder to recognize that influence. Ultimately, what this means is that people in positions of power need to work even harder to make themselves aware of, and to take responsibility for, how their words and actions impact others. How can they do this? Better yet, how can all of us do this? This is what we will turn to in the last chapter.

7

SEEING, FEELING, AND EXPERIENCING YOUR INFLUENCE OVER OTHERS

AS I WRITE THIS BOOK, I am under New York State stay-at-home orders with my two young children and husband as a result of the COVID-19 crisis. I find time to write while my two-year-old naps and my six-year-old is allowed to plug into an iPad for far too long. We are certainly among the fortunate ones: we have been able to work remotely, have kept our jobs, and we have thus far managed to stay healthy. Others have been far less lucky, losing jobs and loved ones, getting sick, being forced to shelter in place in situations where they don't feel safe, and needing to rely on others in ways they never imagined.

Even in the early stages of this crisis, I have already seen so many examples of people underestimating their influence over others. Some of these examples have been infuriating, while others have been heartwarming, but they have all led me to the same conclusion: Never in my lifetime has our inability to see how our behaviors and actions impact others felt so consequential in so many different ways. And never has illuminating our actual influence felt so urgent.

On the infuriating side, even after dire warnings about the need for social distancing, reports continued to come out that people were going out and congregating in groups for frivolous reasons. There were the spring breakers crowding the beaches in Florida,[1] the lines outside pubs in Chicago on Saint Patrick's Day,[2] and the elite Manhattanites posting pictures of themselves flouting bans on nonessential travel on Instagram.[3] While it is easy to dismiss these actions as pure selfishness, I think of them instead as manifestations of everything we've been talking about in this book. As I wrote in an article for *The Hill*, selfishness is being concerned only with one's own outcomes and disregarding others'. A selfish person thinks, "I only care about my own health, and I'm in a low-risk group. I'm not going to abide by social distancing to protect the health of others because I don't care about them."[4] This is not how most people think. Most people do care about other people—more than we tend to give them credit for.[5] A better explanation is that so many people who do things like this are simply oblivious to the impact of their actions on others. They don't want to hurt others—I don't think they were actually prioritizing having a green beer on Saint Patrick's Day over someone else's life—they just weren't attuned to the consequences their actions might hold for someone else. The flurry of seemingly heartfelt apologies and mea culpas that have followed each of these instances seems to support this explanation.[6,7]

On the other hand, there have also been heartwarming examples of people who have underestimated their influence in both significant and delightfully charming ways. One woman, Rebecca Mehra, posted on social media about her experience of being asked by an elderly couple in a grocery store parking lot if she would go in and buy their groceries for them because they were too worried about catching the virus to go in themselves. When she wrote on Twitter about this experience, which "just felt like a no-brainer thing to do in the moment," the response to her story was overwhelming. Many people said her story moved them to look for ways to help at-risk individuals in their own communities. As Mehra said, "It seems like it's inspired thousands of people hopefully to check in on their neighbors, check in on their grandparents, and their parents."[8]

Many people have been surprised at how willing others have been to agree not only to requests for essentials such as food and masks, but also to requests for things that might simply bring them some needed joy, such as sharing a celebration while in quarantine. A North Carolina mother posted a message on a Jeep forum asking a few neighbors to drive by her house for her Jeep-obsessed eight-year-old's birthday. Her post said, "Even if only one Jeep showed up to drive by, this mom would appreciate it more than you could know!" More than a hundred Jeeps ended up driving by.[9]

My colleague Gillian Sandstrom, a psychologist at the University of Essex, had a similar experience when she got an idea for how she wanted to spend her quarantined birthday. After attending a livestream concert online, she thought of how amazing it would be to invite her favorite jazz singer, Sara Dowling, to perform a private remote concert for her birthday. She didn't know if it was plausible, or if the singer would have any interest. As Gillian said to me, "I had no idea if she would do it. I was very nervous sending the email. I didn't even tell my husband until Sara replied." But Gillian ended up asking and was overjoyed when her favorite singer agreed to do it. Not only did it turn out to be a memorable birthday gift for her, but when she invited some friends, it ended up being a way to raise some funds for the singer, whose normally busy gig schedule was suddenly empty for the foreseeable future.

Given everything we've talked about so far, none of these examples should be that surprising. We've already seen how we underestimate the number of people who see the things we post on social media, the likelihood that people will agree to the things we ask for, and how many people copy the things they see us do. The pandemic may have highlighted the urgency of these miscalculations, but they've been there all along.

The lingering question as we come to the end of this book is what to do about it. What is the best way to illuminate our own influence over others, which often seems invisible to us? How can you feel more confident about asking not only for the things you need, but also things that might make your life easier, or bring you some joy? At the same time, how can you become more attuned to the ways in which you may unintentionally impact people by making them uncomfortable or making their lives harder?

Psychologists have spent decades trying to find effective ways of making people more aware of biases like this. I wish I could say that once you're aware of a bias, it goes away, and so, by reading this book, the problem is solved. Unfortunately, it doesn't seem to be that simple.[10] Being aware is certainly a start. But to truly comprehend our influence over others, we must go a bit further.

In this final chapter, I will offer some research-based strategies to help you become more aware of your influence over others. My goal is to help you gain greater awareness of your influence so that you can exercise this untapped influence when it would be helpful to both you and others to do so, and pull back from it when it would not. To help you do this, I've organized this chapter into three main goals, and I will review strategies for achieving each of them. These three goals are for all of us to get better at *seeing*, *feeling*, and *experiencing* our influence over others:

1. The first goal is to start to *see* the impact of our actions on others. In order to do this, we need to get out of our own heads. When we peer out at the world through our own eyes, we don't see ourselves or the role we play in creating the situations we are in. We will explore some strategies for getting out of our own heads so that we can see the role we play in shaping the world and people around us.

2. The second goal is to truly *feel* the impact of our actions. Once we are outside of our own heads, we may be able to see the things we do that impact others, but that doesn't mean we fully appreciate their impact. To do that, we need to get inside other people's heads. We must get better at predicting and understanding how others might feel, as a result of the things we do and say.

3. The third and final goal is to actually *experience* our influence. This aim comes from watching the dramatic transformation participants in my studies have had after being instructed to go out and ask people for things and realizing how much easier it is than they anticipated, and also hearing others' accounts of having similar transformations. However, as we will see, accurately learning about your own influence through direct experience turns out not to be as simple as it may initially seem.

In fact, it is important to clarify that none of these strategies is a magic bullet. As I review the research, we'll see that these suggestions don't work for everyone all of the time. There will be significant caveats along the way. Sometimes these strategies can backfire. At the same time, we will also see that some of the simplest and easiest strategies to implement, such as a seven-minute writing exercise, or simply asking someone else what they are thinking, can have some of the biggest effects. This ultimately makes the prospect of gaining insight into your own influence that much more promising.

SEEING YOUR INFLUENCE ON OTHERS: GETTING OUT OF YOUR OWN HEAD

Take a moment to reflect on a particularly heated argument you have had with a friend or loved one. Try to really put yourself back there and remember all the little details you can—where you were, what was said, the way you said it.

As you re-create this scenario, chances are you have mentally time traveled right back into the head of your past self, looking out through your own eyes. Researchers who have studied the point of view we tend to take when recalling our personal memories have found that when we recall interpersonal interactions such as these, we are most likely to recall them from the first-person perspective. Participants asked to recall a recent conversation, a time when they felt angry, or an embarrassing incident were more than twice as likely to recall each of these kinds of events from the first-person perspective than from any other (e.g., from the perspective of an onlooker, or, even less likely, from the other party's perspective).[11]

It makes sense that we would recall these sorts of events primarily in this way. After all, this is the perspective through which we experience the vast majority of events in our lives.

It is rare, though not unheard of, to experience an event from "outside your own body."* However, if you want to become more aware of the impact you have on others, there is a fundamental problem with seeing, remembering, and interpreting the world solely through this first-person perspective: When we look out at the world from inside our own heads, what we don't see is ourselves.

What this means is that when we recall that argument we had with a friend and find ourselves right back inside our own head in that heated moment, we can easily visualize and re-create all of the annoying things our friend did. However, from that same vantage point, it is much more difficult to visualize and re-create all of the annoying things *we* did—things our friend was probably reacting to. This means that our default way of seeing the world can make us oblivious to our own role in eliciting others' behavior. As a result, we may attribute an outburst during an argument to the other person's bad temper, rather than to the infuriating thing we ourselves said. Or, we may attribute a person's enthusiastic nodding along to a diatribe we've gone off on to their own agreement with what we are saying, rather than the inevitable awkwardness that would ensue if they were to disagree with us in that moment.

A classic study by psychologists Daniel Gilbert and Ned Jones reveals just how bad we are at recognizing the role we play in eliciting others' behavior.[12] In their study, participants (called "inducers") were told they would be asking another participant (called the "responder") a series of questions that

---

* And, actually, we are more likely to recall events like giving a public presentation or performance—circumstances where we are already highly aware of being watched by others—from a third-party perspective.

could be answered in either a politically liberal or a politically conservative way (e.g., "Should abortion be legal or illegal?"). Crucially, all of the participants were informed that the responder wouldn't actually be responding to any of these questions with their own opinions. Rather, the responder would say whatever the inducer told them to say, which had been predetermined by the experimenter.

Inducers were given a sheet of paper with two responses to each question—a liberal response, and a conservative response—and were told that the responder had a copy of the same sheet of paper. They would then ask a question, and press a button that indicated to the responder which of the two responses they should read off the paper.

What the researchers were interested in seeing is whether inducers, despite knowing that they had specifically directed the responders to answer these questions in a particular way, still took the responders' answers as indicators of their true political beliefs. To test this, they had half of the participants instruct their responders to give predominantly liberal answers and the other half instruct their responders to give predominantly conservative answers. Then they asked the inducers what they thought the responder's actual political attitudes were.*

What they found is that participants who had instructed responders to respond in more liberal ways subsequently believed those responders actually held more politically liberal views, whereas those who had instructed responders to respond

---

* Unbeknownst to the inducers, there were no actual responders. Instead, a prerecorded response played from behind the wall of a booth in the lab where the fictional responder was supposed to be. As far as the inducers knew, however, another participant in the experiment was reading the answers they themselves were instructing that person to read.

in more conservative ways in turn thought those responders were actually more conservative. Despite the fact that they had complete control over the other person's responses, they still attributed those responses to something about the other person.

When we view the world from inside our own heads, we see only what the people around us are doing—not what we are doing that might be causing them to behave in a particular way. The participants in this study took the responses they heard at face value, and failed to account sufficiently for the ways in which they themselves had elicited those responses.

A natural follow-up question, then, is whether visualizing this scene from a different vantage point—for example, as a third-party observer—would help an inducer become more aware of their influence on the other person. While Gilbert and Jones didn't find support for this in their study, in the decades since, a number of findings have emerged that suggest there may be something to this possibility. More recent research suggests that attempting to visualize an interaction from a third-party perspective may help us to get out of our own heads so that we can see the broader context within which an event is unfolding. This may in turn help us to better recognize the impact of our actions on others.

The third-party perspective is sometimes described as being "a fly on the wall" or the "God's-eye view." Such descriptions drive home the point that this is purely a visual perspective. You aren't adopting the perspective of any particular person—in fact, you don't have to think of yourself as a person at all. It is merely a way of visually representing a scene so that you are seeing both you and whomever you are interacting with.

A number of studies have shown that visualizing a scene from this third-party perspective changes the way we make meaning out of the events we imagine or experience.[13] When we think about an event from the first-person perspective, we tend to pay attention to the concrete details—the specific actions and sensations we imagine or remember taking place in that moment. However, when we think of an event from a third-party perspective, we tend to pay more attention to the abstract meaning of what we are doing—the broader context within which our actions are taking place.

For example, if I asked you to picture yourself voting on election day from the first-person perspective, you might think about things like driving to your polling place, waiting in line, or marking your candidate's name on the ballot—the specific, concrete actions associated with voting. However, if I were to ask you to picture yourself voting on election day from a third-person perspective, you might think more about things like how you are influencing an election, making your opinion heard, and fulfilling your civic duty.[14]

In other words, by picturing yourself from this third-party perspective, you would be more likely to think about how your behavior fits into the larger context, and thus how it influences the people and systems around you. And because you would be more likely to recognize the impact your vote could make, and the value of making that drive and waiting in that line, you might in turn be more likely to exercise the influence you have by voting. Indeed, in one study by psychologist Lisa Libby and colleagues, participants who pictured themselves voting from a third-party perspective the night before an election (the 2004 US presidential election) were more likely to vote in the election the next day than those who pictured themselves voting from a first-person perspective.[15]

This same logic applies to the visual perspective we adopt

when we interact with other people. Recall the heated argument you had with a friend or loved one that you pictured earlier. While most of us default to picturing such arguments from the first-person perspective, it turns out that training ourselves to think about this kind of argument from a third-party perspective has major benefits for our relationships. Eli Finkel, psychologist and author of *The All-or-Nothing Marriage*, and his colleagues found that an intervention in which couples were instructed to try their best to take a neutral third-party perspective* during interactions—particularly disagreements—with their partners were able to maintain greater marital satisfaction over the course of the two-year study than couples who were not instructed to do so.[16]

These researchers argued that their intervention helped to disrupt the chain of negativity that so often occurs during heated arguments. Adopting a third-party perspective helps us to see the bigger picture in which a criticism or concern is being raised, so that rather than simply trading barbs, we can better listen to our partner's underlying concerns. We can see the larger, more nuanced point being made behind a potentially hurtful statement, and consider the consequences of how we choose to respond. This ultimately means we are less likely to simply react or lash out in anger, and more likely to hear what the other person is really saying and consider how our response might impact the other person and our relationship.[17,18]

The intervention Finkel and his colleagues used was incredibly simple. It was a series of writing prompts that took

---

* Technically, participants were told to adopt the "perspective of a neutral party who wants the best for all involved." However, since there was no other intervention condition, the importance of the "best for all involved" part of this instruction is unclear.

participants seven minutes to complete. They completed this intervention three times over the course of a year, for a total of just twenty-one minutes. And yet, something so quick and simple significantly improved the quality of people's marriages in a randomized study.

What other things might this sort of intervention improve? Could taking a few minutes regularly to reflect on our everyday experiences from a third-party perspective help us become more aware of our influence over other people more generally? Would we become more accurate in estimating how many people notice us over the course of a day if we visualized ourselves on our daily commute from a third-person perspective? Would we more accurately determine how many people are likely to agree to our requests for help, or less innocent requests? Would we think more carefully about how our actions (e.g., voting, congregating in groups) fit into the broader social context (e.g., systemic social problems, the spread of a deadly virus)? Would we be more careful about what we post on social media?

We spend so much time in our own heads looking out. As a result, our default mode of attention is to focus on how other people impact us—all of those other bad drivers on the road, the annoying people talking loudly at the table next to you, the germs left on the door from someone else's hands. It's harder for us to recognize when we ourselves have cut someone off with our own driving, when our boisterous conversation is annoying the people at the next table over, or that the germs could be spreading from our own hands. Finkel and his colleagues' intervention offers a promising way to see how our actions are connected to others' and the role we ourselves play in a situation.

Getting out of our own heads is the first step to becoming

more aware of our influence over others. Yet while trying to reflect on situations from a third-party perspective may make it easier for us to see this influence, it doesn't necessarily help us to feel it—to truly understand how other people are impacted by us. That requires an additional step, which is moving from a third-party perspective to the perspective of the person or people being impacted, getting inside their heads, and feeling what they feel.

FEELING YOUR INFLUENCE ON OTHERS: GETTING PERSPECTIVE, NOT TAKING PERSPECTIVE

To truly understand our influence over others, we must not only see the ways in which our actions impact others, but we also then need to be able to understand how those actions actually *feel* to others. Taking a step back and visualizing our actions from a third-party perspective might, for example, help us to recognize the power dynamic at play if we were to ask a subordinate out on a date. However, unless we truly appreciate how awkward and uncomfortable our subordinate would feel refusing us in that moment, we may still fail to appreciate the full extent of the pressure we are putting on them. While we may recognize that there is a power dynamic, and choose to acknowledge or confront it in some way, our attempt to do so may ultimately be inadequate—for example, believing any unintended pressure will magically vanish if we simply preface our request with, "Don't feel obligated, but. . . ."

Once we have gotten out of our own heads, we need to do something else: Get into other people's heads. We must find a way to understand how they are experiencing our presence, words, and actions. Unfortunately, this turns out to be more difficult than most of us think.

It is widely believed that to better understand someone else's thoughts and feelings, we should simply try harder to think about things from their perspective. We should do our best to put ourselves in their shoes. This approach has been endorsed by none other than Dale Carnegie, author of the 1936 blockbuster *How to Win Friends and Influence People*, who counseled in that very book that we should "try honestly to see things from the other person's point of view."[19,20]

Indeed, many people believe this to be an effective exercise. In one study, survey respondents were asked whether they believed someone who was instructed to try to put themselves in another person's shoes would do a better job judging that person's feelings and preferences than someone who was given no such instruction. The majority of respondents—68%—thought that simply trying to take someone else's perspective would make someone better at doing so.[21]

However, it turns out that simply trying to understand another person doesn't actually help us to understand them any better. In a series of studies, psychologists Tal Eyal, Mary Steffel, and Nicholas Epley—the researchers who conducted the above survey—tested whether simply instructing people to try to take another person's perspective made them any more accurate at judging others' thoughts and feelings than people who received no such instruction. Across their twenty-five studies, comprising more than 2,600 participants, they found that actively trying to consider someone else's viewpoint didn't actually make people any better at understanding that person's feelings, attitudes, or preferences.

In these studies, participants were asked to make various judgments about other people—for example, whether someone's smile was genuine, whether they were feeling angry or afraid, whether they were lying or telling the truth, what kinds of movies or jokes they liked, and a number of other tasks where being able to get inside someone else's head would be extremely helpful. Some participants made judgments of strangers, others made judgments of people they knew. Some participants made guesses from photos, while others actually interacted with another person. None of these details mattered. Across the board, participants who were explicitly instructed to put themselves in another person's shoes and to actively consider what the other person was thinking and feeling fared no better at any of these tasks than participants who were not given this instruction.

In other words, simply trying to take other people's perspectives does little to give you a more accurate representation of how others see the world. This means it is also unlikely to give you a more accurate understanding of how other people view *you*, and your role in their world.

Here it is worth noting that trying to consider things from another person's point of view isn't an entirely pointless endeavor. This exercise can help us to empathize with other people,[22] motivate us to cooperate with other people,[23] and can even reduce prejudice.[24] These are major benefits. However, if our goal is accuracy—getting to the truth of what someone else thinks, and particularly what they think about us—perspective-taking doesn't offer much.

Why not? Because when we take someone else's perspective, try as we might to imagine the world from that person's viewpoint, we never actually get out of our own heads. The "perspective" that emerges is based solely on our own ideas about what that person is likely to be thinking and feeling. For example, if I were to ask you to imagine how someone would feel if you went up and complimented them, you would use your own ideas about how that experience would unfold to imagine how the other person would feel. And, as we saw at the beginning of this book, you would probably be wrong. Try as you may to take the other person's perspective, you would be anchored to your own assumptions about how annoyed and bothered *you* think the other person would feel.

If taking someone else's perspective isn't useful for getting inside their heads and understanding what they are really thinking and feeling—particularly how they might be thinking and feeling about us—what might be more useful? While these researchers found that *taking* perspective doesn't bring us any closer to understanding others' internal worlds, it turns out that *getting* perspective does. As they explain it, the main difference between taking someone's perspective and getting perspective is whether you are exposed to new information. Taking someone's perspective is really about what we presume someone else's feelings to be, rather than what someone else's feelings actually are. But *getting* perspective requires gathering additional information about another person's actual thoughts and feelings.

An extremely straightforward, and effective, way to get perspective is to simply ask someone what they are thinking or feeling. Even though people don't always tell us exactly what they are thinking, or even necessarily know how they truly feel about something, talking to another person gets you out of the echo chamber of your own head. It allows you to base your reading of someone else's mind on more than just your own assumptions about them. And, as we saw in Chapter 5, people are more willing than we think to share personal information.

To demonstrate the effectiveness of this strategy, Eyal and her coauthors added a new condition to the final study in their twenty-five-study research project and enlisted romantic couples to participate. Participants were asked to guess how their significant other would respond to a series of opinion questions, such as "I have somewhat old-fashioned tastes and habits," and "I am a homebody," on a scale from 1 (strongly disagree) to 7 (strongly agree). Importantly, before guessing how their partner would respond, participants were either instructed to imagine seeing the world through their partner's eyes (the perspective-taking condition) or to ask their partner directly what their opinions were on these different statements (the perspective-getting condition). Then participants in both conditions indicated how they thought their partner would respond to each item on the provided seven-point scale.

Not surprisingly, participants who actually talked to their partners about their opinions were much more accurate at guessing the exact rating their partners would give on the scale than those who simply tried to imagine the world from their partner's perspective. What *was* surprising, however, is that although participants who simply tried to take their partner's perspective and didn't actually consult with their partner about their answers were less accurate, they were just as confident in their ability to guess their partner's ratings as those who had talked to their partners directly about these very items.

What this means is that while this finding may seem obvious in theory, it isn't obvious in practice. Of course we are better judges of what someone else thinks if they have already told us what they think. Yet we fail to recognize the clear superiority of this strategy. We think searching our own minds is just as effective for understanding what someone else is thinking and feeling as actually probing that person's mind.

The difficulty of getting into others' heads, and our inability to recognize the limitations of trying to do so via perspective-taking alone, are major reasons why we underestimate our influence over others. Our expectations of how others are likely to respond to our pitches and pleas are based on our own assumptions about their motivations and feelings—assumptions that are often inaccurate, but about which we feel confident. Although we may feel quite strongly that someone will say "no" to our request or be bothered by our compliment, as we have seen, we are largely wrong about how others are likely to react in both cases.

To truly understand the impact of our influence, we can't just guess—we must proactively gather external information. As Eyal and her coauthors put it, "interpersonal understanding may come most readily from becoming a more effective questioner and listener, like a skilled journalist or a survey interviewer, rather than by trying to become a routine perspective taker."[25]

At times we may feel like this process of questioning and listening is unnecessary. We may be quite confident that we already know what someone else is thinking and feeling. This is particularly the case if we ourselves have been in a similar situation. We may believe that our shared experience offers some special access into another person's head and insight into their inner character.

And, indeed, sometimes shared experiences do provide unique insight. For example, in the study of unwanted romantic advances I described in Chapter 5, Lauren DeVincent and I found that individuals who had previously rejected a co-worker's unwanted romantic advances were better able to appreciate how awkward it would be for a co-worker to reject *their* advances.[26] In other words, they were able to draw from their own previous experiences in this role, and it helped them to better appreciate the thoughts and feelings of the person they were romantically interested in—and consequently how their actions might impact that person.

But while drawing from your own experiences can sometimes be an effective way of getting perspective, researchers have identified some important caveats, which demonstrate how this is not always the case. In fact, because people can experience similar events in very different ways, sometimes drawing from your own experience to infer another person's experience can backfire.

For instance, when I talk about those same unwanted romantic advances findings, I find that I often get the kind of reaction described above: Individuals (primarily women) who have been in the awkward position of being hit on by a boss or co-worker and having to reject them will say that my findings ring true and that they hope workplace reforms, such as banning relationships between bosses and subordinates, will continue. However, there is another type of reaction I frequently get as well: Individuals who have been in the position of being hit on by a boss or co-worker, who then went on to marry, have kids with, and live happily ever after with that person. Those people instead tend to lament that banning relationships between bosses and subordinates will mean the end of workplace romance. These two types of individuals have had similar experiences, but those experiences took very different turns, and depending on the turn any particular individual's experience took, they may have very different ideas about what someone might think or feel in response to being hit on by their boss.

These anecdotal examples reveal how sharing a common experience can sometimes make us more attuned to others' thoughts and feelings, yet other times can make us less so. This is an observation that is consistent with research by Rachel Ruttan, Mary-Hunter McDonnell, and Loran Nordgren. These researchers examined situations in which having a similar past experience actually makes a person less understanding of what someone else is going through.[27]

In one study, they had participants read about a high school student who was being bullied in the cafeteria. The student was either described as enduring this hurtful experience, or losing control and lashing out violently at the aggressors and other nearby students. After reading one of these two descriptions, participants rated how compassionate they felt toward the student and how much they liked and thought positively of the student.

The researchers also collected information about the participants' personal histories with bullying, so they were able to assess whether having had a past experience of being bullied made people more compassionate toward the bullied student. It turns out that participants who had endured high school bullying themselves were more compassionate toward the bullied student, and evaluated him more highly than participants who had no such experience. However, this was only true when the student was described as *enduring* the bullying. When the student was described instead as lashing out, the reverse was true—participants who had previously endured bullying themselves were *less* compassionate and evaluated him *more* negatively than those who hadn't had a similar experience with bullying.

Personal experience can indeed help you to better understand someone else's perspective—but only if their way of responding to an experience mirrors yours. We tend to assume that others will react to things the way we would react or have reacted in the past, but that assumption is often false.[28] This brings us back to the value of simply asking. Trying to understand how someone else feels by drawing from your own previous experiences is still in many ways the same as trying to figure out what is in someone else's mind by searching your own. You are still presuming to know what someone else is thinking and feeling, rather than actually knowing what they are thinking and feeling. The problem is that you may feel even more confident in the inaccurate image you've conjured up precisely because you have been through something similar yourself. The only way to know whether you are correct is to gather information from outside your head. Just ask.

What this means for understanding our influence over others is that if we truly want to understand our influence over other people, we must listen to other people. We need to hear their stories rather than just draw from our own stories, or the stories we've created about them. Ideally, we would do this by conversing directly with people we have impacted, or are hoping to impact, but this is not always possible. For every experience like Aziz Ansari's in which you wake up to a text outlining in precise detail how your actions impacted someone else in ways you were unaware of, there are many more such instances that go unsaid. Further, waiting for others to speak up and tell us how we have impacted them places the burden on *them*, which, as we have seen, can be both unrealistic and unfair. All of this means we need to find other ways of listening to other people's experiences. We need to read all of those powerful Me

Too stories, the crushing stories of racial discrimination shared by Black, Indigenous, and other people of color, and the heart-breaking stories of healthcare workers battling COVID-19 in the epicenter of the outbreak. We must listen to these stories, even when—and especially when—they make us sad or uncomfortable, or we will never understand how deeply our words and actions can impact others. It is through listening that we can get perspective.

EXPERIENCING YOUR INFLUENCE ON OTHERS: REJECTION THERAPY

Jason Comely was working as a tech freelancer when his wife left him for "someone that was taller" and "had more money."[29] In the months following that painful rejection, he stopped going out and talking to people. Isolated and depressed, he ended up having a crying breakdown that he now looks back on as a turning point in his life. At that point, he decided that his fear of being rejected again had led him to become socially incapacitated, and he set out to do something about it.

At the time, Comely had been reading about the Spetsnaz, a Russian special ops unit known for its intense training exercises, and he decided that managing his fear of rejection required the same sort of military approach. He made a rule for himself that he had to get rejected every day until he vanquished his fear of rejection. He started small, for example, asking a stranger for a mint. But as should come as no surprise to us by now, he soon learned that he needed to up the ante to get his daily dose of rejection. So, he came up with more and more ridiculous things to ask people: He would ask a stranger to compliment him, a random person to race him, a waitress to dance with him.

Over the course of this "therapy," which actually closely resembles a real therapeutic approach for confronting phobias known as exposure therapy,[30] Comely came to believe that he had inoculated himself against rejection. He was happier, and more confident. Thinking that others might similarly benefit from his approach, he went back through the many rejections he had accumulated over the course of his "treatment" and had them printed onto a deck of cards. He turned "Rejection Therapy" into a card game.

The game really took off when an aspiring entrepreneur, Jia Jiang, stumbled upon it while searching the internet for strategies to conquer his own fear of rejection. Jiang documented his progression through the game on his blog, *100 Days of Rejection Therapy*, complete with videos of all 100 of his rejections. On his blog, you can see Jiang getting rejected by a manager at Costco after asking if he could speak over the Costco intercom, by a FedEx worker after asking if he could FedEx a package to Santa Claus, and by a groomer at PetSmart who declined a request to trim his hair.

While people may have come to Jiang's blog for the schadenfreude of watching someone get rejected, part of its popularity was most certainly that so many of his encounters are actually quite heartwarming. When people reject him, they are polite, even cheerful. The Costco manager cordially explains why he can't let Jiang speak over the intercom, and then tells him to order whatever he wants from the store restaurant on the house.[31] The FedEx worker tries with the utmost sincerity to come up with solutions to Jiang's Santa Claus dilemma.[32] The PetSmart groomer looks bemused in the video, but also genuinely torn because she wants to help him out, but it is against store policy to cut human hair.[33]

And then there are all the things people say "yes" to. A police officer lets him sit in the driver's seat of his police car.[34] People tell him he's tall, nice looking, and has nice hair after he asks them for compliments.[35] A Krispy Kreme employee goes above and beyond to solve the problem of linking five donuts together to make them look like the Olympic rings.[36]

Throughout his blog journey, you can see Jiang have the same revelation that I've seen so many of the participants in my lab studies come to: People are more likely to agree to do things for you than you think—even weird, time-consuming things. When describing his Olympic ring donut request in a TEDx Talk years later, Jiang marveled of the request, "there's no way they could say yes, right?" Expressing how touched he was by the effort the donut maker put into his project, he said, "I just couldn't believe it." Not only that, Jiang goes on, "That video got over five million views on YouTube. The world couldn't believe that either."[37]

Jiang is a convert. He even acquired the trademark rights to the Rejection Therapy name, began publishing a blog called *Rejection Therapy with Jia Jiang* and giving Rejection Therapy seminars, and wrote a book about his experience called *Rejection Proof*. Through this process, Jiang has certainly become more aware of his own influence. He realized, he says in his TEDx Talk, that he "could fulfill [his] life dreams just by simply asking." And he thinks everyone should do this.

Is he right? Is the key to understanding our influence simply to go for it and see what happens? I'll admit, I find the idea of Rejection Therapy extremely appealing. From Comely's, Jiang's, and many others' experiences, the learning curve seems to be steep, and the takeaways appear transformative. It also fits with what I've seen in my own lab. In fact, I first learned about Rejection Therapy from a participant in one of my studies. It was one of the studies where participants ask strangers to vandalize library books. The participant contacted me afterward to set up a meeting to chat about the study. I was worried he was going to interrogate me on the ethics of asking people to vandalize library books, but instead he asked me if the study was related to this thing called Rejection Therapy, to which I admitted it was not, and that I'd never heard of it.

Although I hadn't heard of Rejection Therapy, that wasn't the first—or last—time someone had suggested that taking part in one of my studies is equivalent to an intervention that changes the way they see and experience their own influence. There seems to be some truth to that. People expect the task of asking people for whatever it is I've instructed them to ask for to be awful, go out and get more yesses than they had expected, and have a sort of "aha" moment. But as tempting as it may be to conclude that the best way to gain insight into your influence over others is to put yourself out there and test drive the influence you have, I have my doubts about this approach as the be-all and end-all.

For one, I wonder how universal the takeaways garnered from this approach are likely to be. Would it really work for everyone? Jason Comely, Jia Jiang, and the participant in my study who introduced me to Rejection Therapy are all white or Asian, and male. How widely are their experiences likely to generalize? Would it work for members of demographic groups who have experienced what is essentially systemic, institution-alized rejection, as is the case for many people of color? What about for members of groups who have historically been feared and punished for exercising their own power and influence, such as Black Americans? Unfortunately, because many experi-mental psychologists rely on convenience samples of university

181

students to participate in their studies, and these samples tend to be overwhelmingly white, the answers to these questions are open. We simply don't have the data to know how someone's race might systematically change the outcome of this sort of exercise. In fact, this is the case for many of the findings I've described throughout this book. An overreliance on white participants is a major and long-standing limitation of much of psychological research.[38]

Another question is how gender might impact a person's experience with something like Rejection Therapy. Women often hold back from asking for things out of valid concerns with being disapproved of or disliked, a phenomenon examined in detail in Linda Babcock and Sara Laschever's fantastic book, *Women Don't Ask*.[39] Might women approach this sort of forced exercise by asking differently, or draw different insights from it?

A little while ago, I had an opportunity to reflect on this question. I was invited to participate in a BBC show called *My Name Is . . .*, which tells a different story in each episode of "an individual with a story to tell, and some answers to find, in today's Britain." The episode I was involved in was called "Hayley: Asking for Rejection," and it was about "a young woman who wants to get better at dealing with rejection and asking for what she wants without fear of No."[40] As part of the episode, Hayley essentially embarks on a day-long Rejection Therapy session.

Hayley's first attempt at rejection looks much like Jiang's. She asks a vendor at a food market for a pear, "Excuse me, mate? Can I have this pear?" "Yeah," he says without missing a beat. As Hayley replies, "Lovely, thank you," her producer, Meara, can be heard laughing in the background, gleefully and breathlessly saying, "Oh my God. He said, he said yes!" Hayley's next two requests, for a parsnip and an herbal deodorant from two more vendors at the same market, don't go as well and she gets her first "no." But the herbalist is endlessly apologetic, saying: "I wish I could . . . ," and "If it was my shop . . ."

After another request, to take a tour of someone's boat, is denied because the owner says the boat isn't clean enough for guests, Hayley and her producer note, "It was hard for her [the boat owner] to say no." Jiang had noted something similar in his rejection attempts, saying after he had asked people for compliments that it had been "harder [for them] to reject giving compliments than to agree."[41] But here is where Hayley and Jiang's experiences diverge in interesting and illuminating ways.

Following the observation that is it hard for people to say "no," Jiang nonetheless declares assuredly, "We should all try this." What he is learning from this experience, after all, is that the way to reach all of your goals is simply to ask.

Hayley's takeaway from this observation, on the other hand, is quite different. Immediately after noting how hard it was for the boat owner to say "no," she reflects, "I guess you got to read that, and not push." Later in the podcast, Hayley is talking to a friend about her experience and the conversation turns to how important it is to give people space to feel comfortable rejecting you. "Never stand between a woman and the door, literally or metaphorically," her friend muses. While Jiang looked back at the times people hesitated to agree in order to figure out what he could have done differently to get a "yes," Hayley reflected on these moments as opportunities to make it easier for someone to say "no."

These two takeaways couldn't be more different. While both individuals came to recognize the power of their own influence through this experience, one took that as permission to use that influence more, while one took it as a reason to take a step back and give people more space—essentially, to use their influence less. As we've seen, both of these conclusions are valid. In an ideal world, a person would have both of these insights. However, at least in these two anecdotal incidences, the takeaways people are drawing from these experiences seem to lean more one way than the other, and the direction seems to be gendered.

I don't want to make too much of these two individual cases. There are certainly women whose experiences with Rejection Therapy look very similar to Jiang's. In a *Harper's Bazaar* article, one female writer wrote of her experience with Rejection Therapy (in a sentence that could have been written by Carrie Bradshaw herself) that the process made her realize that "life can change the moment you stop making excuses and do the things that scare you."[42] I also don't typically find gender differences in the studies I've run that are most similar to Rejection Therapy. Women and men who have asked strangers for favors in my studies have for the most part underestimated the likelihood people would agree to those requests to a similar degree.[43]

On the other hand, the contrast between what Jiang and what Hayley learned from their experiences with Rejection Therapy is consistent with the gender differences I have found in my unwanted romantic advances studies—a domain where men and women tend to have very different histories. As noted above, women in those studies were more aware of the pressure they put on others whom they were romantically interested in because of how often they had found themselves in similar situations. Their own previous experience in the role of being the target of unwanted advances helped them to better appreciate the thoughts and feelings of the person they were romantically interested in when it turned out that person didn't return their interest.

Ultimately, I can't say for sure whether there are systematic differences in how people with different gender or racial identities are likely to experience an exercise like this. But what all of this means to me is that we shouldn't assume the lessons people will learn from such an intervention will be universal. The takeaways of such an experience are most certainly more complex than we might conclude from the accounts of a couple of Rejection Therapy converts. And that isn't the only problem with relying on experience as the primary means of learning about your influence over others.

You may have already wondered at some point in this book: If people are so willing to agree to our requests, why don't we know that already? It's not like anyone can completely avoid asking people for things their whole lives. Most of us have at some point asked for directions, for advice, to borrow a pen, or for someone to hold the door. And we have most likely been told "yes" in each of these instances. Why haven't we learned from these experiences to worry less about asking people for things, like Comely and Jiang seem to have done?

The problem is that we don't always remember these experiences in the most accurate, objective way. As with so many other things in life, the negative looms larger than the positive. Negative events tend to be more salient and leave a longer lasting impression on us than positive events—a phenomenon known as "negativity bias."[44] That means we tend to forget all of those mundane requests that people agreed to, while our memory for every little rejection we've experienced tends to be long and painful.

Hayley fell prey to this tendency when she and her producer took a break from her Rejection Therapy–type session to grab a Guinness at a nearby pub. Sitting at the bar, Hayley's producer asks her if she feels less afraid of rejection. Hayley replies that she feels less optimistic about the human race. "But," her producer chimes in quickly to remind her, "you did get a lot of yesses too. Think about the yesses. You got a free pear, you got some chips. . . ." Hayley acquiesces, saying, "I think this is part of my problem, I just focus on the negatives way too easily."

But this problem isn't specific to Hayley. "Bad is stronger than good" is one of the most reliable effects in social psychology.[45] It is a problem we all seem to share, and it is a substantial part of why we underestimate our influence over others. While we may replay over and over in our minds the time we tried to influence someone and failed, we quickly forget all the times we succeeded.

Another problem with an experiential intervention, such as Rejection Therapy, is that any one exercise could never be broad enough in scope to offer a complete understanding of our own multifaceted influence over others. Yet research shows that getting a tiny taste of a complicated phenomenon can fool us into thinking we understand what that phenomenon is all about. For example, in one study by psychologists Arielle Silverman, Jason Gwinn, and Leaf Van Boven, participants were asked to simulate what it would be like to be blind by completing a series of tasks while blindfolded. Participants who engaged in this brief, crude simulation were subsequently more sympathetic to blind people, which is typically the goal of these sorts of interventions. But at the same time, they also judged blind people to be less capable than participants who were simply asked to imagine what it would be like to be blind.[46] Although the simulators had only experienced a fleeting moment of being unable to see, they extrapolated this experience to their understanding of the actual, long-term process of first becoming and then adapting to and functioning while being blind—and thus had a more negative perception of the capabilities of blind people.*

Just as putting on a blindfold can't tell us about the complex experience of being blind, it would be unrealistic to think that going out and making a handful of wacky requests is likely to be the final say on understanding our influence over others. Asking more may indeed teach us about the power of asking. However, it won't teach us about all of the intricate ways in which we influence others throughout our lives, particularly when we aren't asking for things, and are instead influencing others by modeling behavior, persuading, or simply existing in a space.

Finally, as we've seen, there are instances, such as with romantic advances and inappropriate requests, when it is better to find a way to recognize your influence *without* having to experience it directly. Not only do we not want people going out and asking for things indiscriminately just to test out their own influence in those domains, it is unclear what someone would even learn from doing so. As we've seen, the people you ask may very well smile and comply, all the while wishing they could say "no," but feeling too awkward and uncomfortable to do so. So, you may walk away from such an interaction with a totally different interpretation of what just happened than the other person.

As one example, after taking part in my library book vandalism study, participants would sometimes express their shock at having discovered how unethical people really were. A common sentiment was, "I can't believe how many people are willing to do that!" Of course, we know that many of the people these participants approached weren't willing—they just couldn't find the words to express their unwillingness. But this dynamic

---

* A characterization that certainly isn't helped by cartoons like Mr. Magoo.

was often lost on the people doing the asking. Upon discovering that people were more willing to do unethical things than they thought, these participants thought they had gained some sort of insight into the morality of the human race. But they were in fact missing the most important insight—that it was harder for people to say "no" to *them* than they had thought—and thus their own power to shape others' moral behaviors was greater than they had thought.

To be sure, we didn't let participants walk out of our experiment thinking this. In the debriefing all participants were given at the end of the study, we clued everyone in to the main point of the research. However, this example once again demonstrates the limitations of relying on experience alone for insights about our influence over others.

Despite all of these caveats, I certainly don't want to dismiss the role of experience entirely. (After all, I did make it one of my three primary ways of gaining insight into the influence you have on others.) Under certain circumstances—as in the cases of individuals who have found Rejection Therapy to indeed be utterly transformative—experience can be a powerful tool for appreciating the influence you have. However, we tend to hold up personal experience as the pinnacle of insight, when, as we have seen, experience can be flawed. Our own personal experiences can be misremembered and misinterpreted, which means the things we learn from our experiences don't necessarily represent the ultimate truth.

More than that, simple, straightforward experiential assignments (e.g., "Go out and ask someone for something!"; "Give someone a compliment today!") can indeed teach us about simple, straightforward forms of influence. But that isn't the same thing as learning how to use your influence wisely, for example knowing when to hold back from asking, or to refrain from chiming in on something you don't know enough about. It is harder to learn from experience when the experience is one of inaction, rather than action. This is why, in order to understand the multifaceted nature of your own influence, you need more than just experience—you need to be able to see and feel your influence as well, as we talked about earlier in this chapter.

All of this means that I think you *should* go out today and ask someone for something, or give someone a compliment. But in addition to that, I think you need to get out of your own head, get perspective, and reflect on your experiences.

Even Jia Jiang didn't discover his asking "superpower" through experience alone. In his TEDx Talk, he describes the first request he made as part of his Rejection Therapy experiment. He had to ask someone to borrow $100, so he went down to the lobby of his office building, and asked a security guard sitting behind a desk. "Hey, sir, can I borrow 100 dollars from you?" Jiang asked. "No," was the initial response. Humiliated and embarrassed, Jiang almost missed the security guard's follow-up question: "Why?" At that point, he was so mortified that instead of answering this follow-up question, Jiang just asked, "No?" said "I'm sorry," and ran away.

Jiang's first experience with rejection was awful and humiliating. However, he didn't rely on experience alone to draw conclusions about what had just happened. He also recorded the interaction between himself and the security guard. As he watched the footage later that night, he says, "I was watching myself get rejected, and I just saw how scared I was." But as he continued to watch, his attention turned to the other person and the exchange that occurred between them: "Then I saw this guy. You know, he wasn't that menacing. . . . And he even asked me,

'Why?' In fact, he invited me to explain myself. And I could've said many things. I could've explained, I could've negotiated. I didn't do any of that. All I did was run."[47]

Looking out through his own eyes in the moment, Jiang viewed the experience of rejection as humiliating and terrifying, and the person doing the rejection as menacing. However, when he stepped back and took a third-party perspective— when he was able to watch the interaction between himself and this other person take place, as if he were a fly on the wall—a different dynamic became clear. He saw the willingness of the other person to hear him out. He heard the opportunity for influence embedded in that follow-up question ("Why?"), and he was able to see the influence he had—the influence he had missed in the moment.

Jiang's Rejection Therapy journey is certainly a powerful example of how enlightening experiential interventions can be. But as we just saw it is also a reminder of how we can be misled by over-relying on experience. Experience alone is not enough to gain insight into all of the complex and underappreciated ways you regularly impact other people, for better and worse. For that, you need to see, feel, *and* experience the influence you have.

Conclusion

HALLOWEEN IS MY favorite holiday. I couldn't wait for my kids to get old enough to take them trick-or-treating. My husband, however, has sworn off trick-or-treating since one fateful Halloween night back in the fifth grade. Tall for his age and dressed up in his dad's trench coat and a scary mask, he knocked on a neighbor's door, saying, "Trick or treat!" The neighbor didn't recognize him and growled something along the lines of, "I only give candy to kids." Dejected, my husband went straight home that night, and now tells his sad story every October while explaining why it is his prerogative to stay home and hand out the candy.

We all have thoughts and memories of things other people have said or done that reverberate in our heads and impact our way of thinking and being in enduring ways. One small comment from a neighbor comes back to haunt my husband every Halloween. I can credit some of my most important career decisions, key aspects of my worldview, and the way I take my coffee in part to offhand remarks from colleagues and random encounters with strangers. I still get a boost of assurance from recalling that time a respected senior colleague complimented my research years ago, and I can still remember how bad it felt to be on the receiving end of a particularly grumpy review of one of my first papers.

What I've tried to highlight in this book is that the things we say and do can eventually become the thoughts and memories that reverberate in *other people's* heads. And it doesn't take as much as we think for that to happen.

Throughout this book, we have seen the misperceptions we have about how influence works. We have seen the gap between the things we *think* we need to do in order to have influence, and the things that actually give us influence every single day. We've seen that our mere presence has more impact on others than we realize, that we shouldn't worry so much about saying things perfectly, and that people are more likely to do things for us than we think—as long as we can get up the nerve to ask them directly. But we've also seen how important it is for people to take responsibility for their words and actions, especially when they are in positions of power, precisely *because* people see, hear, process, and do the things we say and do more than we realize.

I hope the tools I have shared here will help you to recognize all of this in your own life. However, it is worth repeating that none of these tools is a magic bullet. Ultimately, you won't know every time someone notices you, thinks about something you said weeks later, or is moved to change their behavior after seeing something you did. You may still underestimate how well your argument came across to someone else. You may continue to miss times where you have asked someone for something that made them uncomfortable. But now you know that all of those things are happening more than you have probably realized. You have more influence than you think—both when you are actively trying to influence others, and when you are not. And all of that unseen influence comes with a lot of unseen responsibility.

As I stated at the beginning of this book, most books about influence and persuasion have one main goal: to make you a more confident and effective influencer. I share this goal—to a point. I hope that I have convinced you that having influence is in many ways easier and less extraordinary than we imagine. While the times you've tried and failed to influence someone may loom large, there are undoubtedly far more examples of times you've influenced someone without trying at all—and without ever seeing the influence you had. I hope that this knowledge indeed makes you a more confident and effective influencer. And I hope that confidence frees you to use your voice to advocate for what you need and what you believe in, as well as to trust that others are hearing and responding to you.

But my goal in writing this book goes beyond that. I also want to help you develop a more nuanced understanding of your influence over others—one that allows you to more accurately recognize the influence you already have, not only so you feel more confident using that influence, but also so you feel more confident *not* using it. Perhaps you need to ask more. But maybe you need to ask less. My hope is that by getting out of your own head, getting perspective, and reflecting on your own experiences, you can learn how to use your unseen influence wisely. If the things we say and do have the potential to reverberate in other people's heads the way they do in ours, we should try to make those things count.

Acknowledgments

IN THE SPIRIT of this book, I have so many people to thank whose friendship, wisdom, and wit have influenced and inspired me in more ways than they could ever know.

First and foremost, I am eternally grateful to my husband, life partner, and best friend, Stephen D'Angelo, whose generous support made it possible to finish this book with two young children at home in the middle of a pandemic—circumstances I admittedly did not anticipate when I began this project.

I owe so much gratitude to my editor, Quynh Do, for her spot-on edits, for whittling down my Taylor Swift references to the optimal number, and for letting me write a somewhat unconventional influence book, and to my agent, Giles Anderson, for his support and direction, for identifying the perfect publisher, and for his willingness to broach the subject of the obvious *Buffy* connection. Thank you both for your patience and insights. Thank you also to Kate Adams for her indispensable advice and edits when this book was in its earliest stages, and to Melanie Tortoroli for holding my hand to the finish line.

Thank you to my wonderful friends and colleagues who read various drafts of the book. Two of the best writers I know, Kirstin Appelt and Dan Newark, read the book carefully cover to cover. Thanks to Dan for nixing my italics and teaching me the correct usage of "peruse" and to Kirstin for her preternatural wordsmithing throughout. Thank you also to Laura Giurge for reading the entire book and coming up with new research ideas on every page, to Rachel Aleks, Bob Frank, and Emily Zitek for giving invaluable feedback on sections of the book, and to my husband for getting two-thirds of the way through.

To the people who have shaped my thinking throughout my career, while modeling how to be great researchers and also caring, fun, multidimensional human beings. My incomparable collaborator, mentor, and friend, Frank Flynn, without whom this book would not exist. My amazing graduate advisor, Tory Higgins. The Higgins Lab. The ExPO Lab. All of my incredible colleagues, collaborators, and mentors over the years.

To the researchers whose work my ideas always seem to begin with, and return back to, Erica Boothby, Bob Cialdini, David Dunning, Nick Epley, Erving Goffman, Tom Gilovich, Adam Grant, Marianne LaFrance, Stanley Milgram, Dale Miller, John Sabini, Roseanna Sommers, Sunita Sah, Leaf Van Boven.

To all the people who shared articles and examples I ended up using in the book, including Natalie Bazarova, Erica Boothby, Brady Butterfield, Brian Earl, René Kizilcec, Alison Ledgerwood, Neil Lewis, Drew Margolin, Dan Newark, Nick Saleh, and Janis Whitlock, and to everyone who let me share their personal stories and insights, including Alex Colvin, Kevin Hallock, Alan Mathios, Naomi Tweyo Nkinsi, Erika Rauer, Gillian Sandstrom, and of course Stephen, Hanna, and Evelyn.

To my current and former students, student collaborators, and research assistants, without whom much of this research would not have been possible, including Hillie Aaldering, Meredith Anderer, Ava Barnett, Sangah Bae, Emily Dawson,

Sebastian Deri, Lauren DeVincent, Lily Ellis, Kelly Jahnsen, Eshaan Jain, Jennifer Logg, Changguo Mao, Amanda Miner, David Navadeh, Courtney Noll, Pierson Ohr, Maya Portillo, Megan Rodriguez, Mahdi Roghanizad, Jeffrey Sherman, Cassidy Shiel, Kendra Sober, Daniel Stein, Carlie Stewart, Harry Trabue, Charlotte Walden, Vicki Xie, and Amy Xu.

To all of the amazing people I've had the fortune of having in my life who have impacted me in ways both large and small, including Keith, Ashley, and Connor Bohns, Sue, Paul, and Sarah D'Angelo, Rachel Aleks, Kirstin Appelt, Kate Bieger, Becky Colesworthy, Lauren Costa, Sanford DeVoe, Allison Elias, Jeremy Goodridge, and Abby Scholer.

To the childcare workers who put my mind at ease so I could concentrate on writing knowing my littles are safe and happy.

To Grandma and Poppy and all of my extended family for their love and support.

And, lastly, to my parents, Steve and Kathy, for everything.

Notes

INTRODUCTION

1. Erica J. Boothby and Vanessa K. Bohns, "Why a simple act of kindness is not as simple as it seems: Underestimating the positive impact of our compliments on others," *Personality and Social Psychology Bulletin* 47, no. 5 (2021): 826-840, https://doi.org/10.1177/0146167220949003.
2. For similar findings when people give compliments to friends, see also Xuan Zhao and Nicholas Epley, "Kind words do not become tired words: Undervaluing the positive impact of frequent compliments," *Self and Identity*, 2020, https://doi.org/10.1080/15298868.2020.1761438, and Xuan Zhao and Nicholas Epley, "Insufficiently complimentary? Underestimating the positive impact of compliments creates a barrier to expressing them," *Journal of Personality and Social Psychology*, 2021 (forthcoming).
3. Amit Kumar and Nicholas Epley, "Undervaluing gratitude: Expressers misunderstand the consequences of showing appreciation," *Psychological Science* 29, no. 9 (2018): 1423–1435, https://doi.org/10.1177/0956797618772506.

CHAPTER 1: UNSEEN INFLUENCE

1. Kenneth P. Vogel, "Isn't that the Trump Lawyer?," *New York Times,* September 19, 2017, https://www.nytimes.com/2017/09/19/us/politics/isnt-that-the-trump-lawyer-a-reporters-accidental-scoop.html.
2. Fred Barbash, "Trump lawyers spill beans, thanks to terrible choice of restaurant," *Washington Post,* September 18, 2017, https://

www.washingtonpost.com/news/morning-mix/wp/2017/09/18/
trump-lawyers-spill-beans-after-terrible-restaurant-choice-next
-to-nyt/?utm_term=.e8c581fa106c.

3. Dana Milbank, "A Trump lawyer caught gabbing about Russia
at lunch racks up career errors," *Washington Post,* September
18, 2017, https://www.washingtonpost.com/opinions/a-trump
-lawyer-caught-gabbing-about-russia-at-lunch-racks-up-career
-errors/2017/09/18/34eea27a-9cbc-11e7-9083-fbfddf6804c2_story
.html?utm_term=.df8c81d8df5c.

4. Erica J. Boothby, Margaret S. Clark, and John A. Bargh, "The invisibility cloak illusion: People (incorrectly) believe they observe others
more than others observe them," *Journal of Personality and Social Psychology* 112, no. 4 (2017): 589, https://doi.org/10.1037/pspi0000082.

5. Chenbo Zhong, Francesca Gino, and I have referred to the sense of
invisibility we experience when wearing sunglasses as the "illusion
of anonymity," and have found that this false sense of anonymity
can even lead people to behave more selfishly and dishonestly.
Chen-Bo Zhong, Vanessa K. Bohns, and Francesca Gino, "Good
lamps are the best police: Darkness increases dishonesty and self-
interested behavior," *Psychological Science* 21, no. 3 (2010): 311–314,
https://doi.org/10.1177/0956797609360754.

6. Clara Colombatto, Yi-Chia Chen, and Brian J. Scholl, "Gaze deflection reveals how gaze cueing is tuned to extract the mind behind
the eyes," *Proceedings of the National Academy of Sciences* (2020,
forthcoming), https://doi.org/10.1073/pnas.2010841117.

7. Thomas Gilovich, Victoria Husted Medvec, and Kenneth Savitsky,
"The spotlight effect in social judgment: An egocentric bias in esti-
mates of the salience of one's own actions and appearance," *Journal of Personality and Social Psychology* 78, no. 2 (2000): 211, https://
doi.org/10.1037/0022-3514.78.2.211.

8. Boothby, Clark, and Bargh, "Invisibility cloak illusion," 589.

9. Erica J. Boothby, Margaret S. Clark, and John A. Bargh, "Shared
experiences are amplified," *Psychological Science* 25, no. 12 (2014):
2209–2216, https://doi.org/10.1177/0956797614551162.

10. Garriy Shteynberg, Jacob B. Hirsh, Adam D. Galinsky, and
Andrew P. Knight, "Shared attention increases mood infusion,"

Journal of Experimental Psychology: General 143, no. 1 (2014): 123, https://doi.org/10.1037/a0031549.

11. Todd Leopold, "Broadway legend grabs phone from texter, laments future," *CNN*, July 9, 2015, https://www.cnn.com/2015/07/09/entertainment/feat-patti-lupone-cell-phone/index.html.

12. Eric Sullivan, "Hannah Gadsby explains why Jerry Seinfeld is wrong about PC culture," *Esquire*, September 12, 2019, https://www.esquire.com/entertainment/tv/a28989896/hannah-gadsby-interview-jerry-seinfeld-pc-culture/.

13. Elizabeth Blair, "Comedy clubs are closed, so to reach audiences, comics have to improvise," NPR, May 7, 2020, https://www.npr.org/2020/05/07/848109182/comedy-clubs-are-closed-so-to-reach-audiences-comics-have-to-improvise.

14. *Comedian*, directed by Christian Charles (Miramax, 2002).

15. Katie Reilly, "Read Hillary Clinton's 'basket of deplorables' remarks about Donald Trump supporters," *Time*, September 10, 2016, https://time.com/4486502/hillary-clinton-basket-of-deplorables-transcript/.

16. Chris Cillizza, "Why Mitt Romney's "47 percent" comment was so bad," *Washington Post*, March 4, 2013, https://www.washingtonpost.com/news/the-fix/wp/2013/03/04/why-mitt-romneys-47-percent-comment-was-so-bad/?utm_term=.42fe4de07d11.

17. Gerald E. Echterhoff, E. Tory Higgins, and Stephan Groll, "Audience-tuning effects on memory: The role of shared reality," *Journal of Personality and Social Psychology* 89, no. 3 (2005): 257, https://doi.org/10.1037/0022-3514.89.3.257.

18. Douglas Kingsbury, "Manipulating the amount of information obtained from a person giving directions" (PhD dissertation, Harvard University, 1968).

19. Robert M. Krauss and Susan R. Fussell, "Perspective-taking in communication: Representations of others' knowledge in reference," *Social Cognition* 9, no. 1 (1991): 2–24, https://doi.org/10.1521/soco.1991.9.1.2.

20. Donn Byrne, *The Attraction Paradigm* (Academic Press, 1971).

21. Manis, Melvin, S. Douglas Cornell, and Jeffrey C. Moore, "Transmission of attitude relevant information through a communication

chain," *Journal of Personality and Social Psychology* 30, no. 1 (1974): 81, https://doi.org/10.1037/h0036639.

22. Seth Meyers, "Trevor Noah was a victim of fake news," *Late Night with Seth Meyers,* September 7, 2017, https://www.youtube.com/watch?v=OLxDnnTpgA0.

23. E. Tory Higgins and William S. Rholes, "'Saying is believing': Effects of message modification on memory and liking for the person described," *Journal of Experimental Social Psychology* 14 (1978), 363–378, https://doi.org/10.1016/0022-1031(78)90032-X.

24. Tamara Keith, "Wikileaks claims to release Hillary Clinton's Goldman Sachs Transcripts," NPR, October 15, 2016, https://www.npr.org/2016/10/15/498085611/wikileaks-claims-to-release-hillary-clintons-goldman-sachs-transcripts.

25. Peter Brown, *The Curious Garden* (Little, Brown Books for Young Readers, 2013).

26. Damon Centola, *How Behavior Spreads: The Science of Complex Contagions*, vol. 3. (Princeton University Press, 2018).

27. Robert H. Frank, "Thy neighbor's solar panels," *The Atlantic,* March 2020, https://www.theatlantic.com/magazine/archive/2020/03/climate-change-peer-pressure/605515/.

28. Bryan Bollinger and Kenneth Gillingham, "Peer effects in the diffusion of solar photovoltaic panels," *Marketing Science* 31, no. 6 (2012): 900–912, http://dx.doi.org/10.1287/mksc.1120.0727.

CHAPTER 2: YOUR POWER OF PERSUASION

1. Sebastian Deri, Shai Davidai, and Thomas Gilovich, "Home alone: Why people believe others' social lives are richer than their own," *Journal of Personality and Social Psychology* 113, no. 6 (2017): 858, https://doi.org/10.1037/pspa0000105.

2. Mark D. Alicke and Olesya Govorun, "The better-than-average effect," in *The Self in Social Judgment*, ed. M. D. Alicke, D. A. Dunning, and J. I. Krueger, 85–106 (Psychology Press, 2005).

3. Nicholas Epley and David Dunning, "Feeling 'holier than thou': Are self-serving assessments produced by errors in self- or social prediction?," *Journal of Personality and Social Psychology* 79, no. 6 (2000): 861, https://doi.org/10.1037/0022-3514.79.6.861.

4. Elanor F. Williams and Thomas Gilovich, "Do people really believe they are above average?," *Journal of Experimental Social Psychology* 44 (2008): 1121–1128, https://doi.org/10.1016/j.jesp.2008.01.002.

5. Ola Svenson, "Are we all less risky and more skillful than our fellow drivers?," *Acta Psychologica* 47, no. 2 (1981): 143–148, https://doi.org/10.1016/0001-6918(81)90005-6.

6. Robinson Meyer, "It's a lonely world: The median Twitter user has 1 measly follower," *The Atlantic*, December 19, 2013, https://www.theatlantic.com/technology/archive/2013/12/its-a-lonely-world-the-median-twitter-user-has-1-measly-follower/282513/.

7. Erica J. Boothby, Gus Cooney, Gillian M. Sandstrom, and Margaret S. Clark, "The liking gap in conversations: Do people like us more than we think?," *Psychological Science* 29, no. 11 (2018): 1742–1756, https://doi.org/10.1177/0956797618783714.

8. Robert B. Cialdini, *Influence: The Psychology of Persuasion*, rev. ed. (Harper Business, 2006).

9. Molly J. Crockett, "Moral outrage in the digital age," *Nature Human Behaviour* 1, no. 11 (2017): 769, https://doi.org/10.1038/s41562-017-0213-3.

10. Laura Stafford, Cynthia S. Burggraf, and William F. Sharkey, "Conversational memory: The effects of time, recall, mode, and memory expectancies on remembrances of natural conversations," *Human Communication Research* 14, no. 2 (1987): 203–229, https://doi.org/10.1111/j.1468-2958.1987.tb00127.x.

11. Thomas Holtgraves, "Conversation, speech acts, and memory," *Memory & Cognition* 36, no. 2 (2008): 361–374, https://link.springer.com/article/10.3758/MC.36.2.361.

12. Ellen J. Langer, Arthur Blank, and Benzion Chanowitz, "The mindlessness of ostensibly thoughtful action: The role of 'placebic' information in interpersonal interaction." *Journal of Personality and Social Psychology* 36, no. 6 (1978): 635, https://doi.org/10.1037/0022-3514.36.6.635.

13. Ibid.

14. Cialdini, *Influence*.

15. M. Anne Britt, C. A. Kurby, S. Dandotkar, and C. R. Wolfe, "I agreed with what? Memory for simple argument claims,"

Discourse Processes 45, no. 1 (2007): 52–84, https://doi.org/10
.1080/01638530701739207.

16. M. Anne Britt and Aaron A. Larson, "Constructing representations of arguments," *Journal of Memory and Language* 48, no. 4 (2003): 794–810, https://doi.org/10.1016/S0749-596X(03)00002-0.

17. Valerie F. Reyna and Charles J. Brainerd, "Fuzzy-trace theory: An interim synthesis," *Learning and Individual Differences*, 7, no. 1 (1995): 1–75, https://doi.org/10.1016/1041-6080(95)90031-4.

18. H. Paul Grice, "Logic and conversation," in *Syntax and Semantics 3: Speech Arts,* ed. Peter Cole and Jerry L. Morgan, 41–58 (Academic Press, 1975).

19. Benedictus de (Baruch) Spinoza, *The Ethics and Selected Letters*, trans. Seymour Feldman, ed. Samuel Shirley (Hackett, 1982). (Original work published in 1677.)

20. David D. Clare and Timothy R. Levine, "Documenting the truth-default: The low frequency of spontaneous unprompted veracity assessments in deception detection," *Human Communication Research* 45, no. 3 (2019): 286–308, https://doi.org/10.1093/hcr/hqz001.

21. Daniel T. Gilbert, Douglas S. Krull, and Patrick S. Malone, "Unbelieving the unbelievable: Some problems in the rejection of false information," *Journal of Personality and Social Psychology* 59, no. 4 (1990): 601–613, https://doi.org/10.1037/0022-3514.59.4.601.

22. Daniel T. Gilbert, Romin W. Tafarodi, and Patrick S. Malone, "You can't not believe everything you read," *Journal of Personality and Social Psychology* 65, no. 2 (1993): 221, https://doi.org/10.1037/0022-3514.65.2.221.

23. Katherine Bischoping, "Gender differences in conversation topics, 1922–1990," *Sex Roles* 28, no. 1–2 (1993): 1–18, http://dx.doi.org/10.1007/BF00289744.

24. Ann Kronrod, Amir Grinstein, and Luc Wathieu, "Mind the gap between needs and wants: Misused assertiveness in well-being communication" (working paper, 2020).

25. Ann Kronrod, Amir Grinstein, and Luc Wathieu, "Go green! Should environmental messages be so assertive?," *Journal of Marketing* 76, no. 1 (2012): 95–102, https://doi.org/10.1509/jm.10.0416.

26. Ijeoma Oluo, *So You Want to Talk about Race* (Seal Press, 2019).

27. Don A. Moore and Paul J. Healy, "The trouble with overconfidence," *Psychological Review* 115, no. 2 (2008): 502, https://doi.org/10.1037/0033-295X.115.2.502.
28. Scott Plous, *The Psychology of Judgment and Decision Making* (McGraw-Hill Book Company, 1993).

CHAPTER 3: JUST BECAUSE YOU ASKED

1. Heidi Grant, *Reinforcements: How to Get People to Help You* (Harvard Business Review, 2018).
2. Vanessa K. Bohns, "(Mis)Understanding our influence over others: A review of the underestimation-of-compliance effect," *Current Directions in Psychological Science* 25, no. 2 (2016): 119–123, https://doi.org/10.1177/0963721415628011.
3. Francis J. Flynn and Vanessa K. B. Lake (Bohns), "If you need help, just ask: Underestimating compliance with direct requests for help," *Journal of Personality and Social Psychology* 95, no. 1 (2008): 128, https://doi.org/10.1037/0022-3514.95.1.128.
4. Ibid.
5. Sebastian Deri, Daniel H. Stein, and Vanessa K. Bohns, "With a little help from my friends (and strangers): Closeness as a moderator of the underestimation-of-compliance effect," *Journal of Experimental Social Psychology* 82 (2019): 6–15, https://doi.org/10.1016/j.jesp.2018.11.002.
6. Daniel A. Newark, Francis J. Flynn, and Vanessa K. Bohns, "Once bitten, twice shy: The effect of a past refusal on expectations of future compliance," *Social Psychological and Personality Science* 5, no. 2 (2014): 218–225, https://doi.org/10.1177/1948550613490967.
7. M. Mahdi Roghanizad and Vanessa K. Bohns, "Ask in person: You're less persuasive than you think over email," *Journal of Experimental Social Psychology* 69 (2017): 223–226, https://doi.org/10.1016/j.jesp.2016.10.002.
8. Vanessa K. Bohns, Daniel A. Newark, and Amy Z. Xu, "For a dollar, would you . . . ? How (we think) money affects compliance with our requests," *Organizational Behavior and Human Decision Processes* 134 (2016): 45–62, https://doi.org/10.1016/j.obhdp.2016.04.004.

9. Hillie Aaldering, "If you need help, just ask: Underestimating helping behavior across cultures" (master's thesis, University of Amsterdam, 2009).

10. Vanessa K. Bohns, Michel J. J. Handgraaf, Jianmin Sun, Hillie Aaldering, Changguo Mao, and Jennifer Logg, "Are social prediction errors universal? Predicting compliance with a direct request across cultures," *Journal of Experimental Social Psychology* 47, no. 3 (2011): 676–680, https://doi.org/10.1016/j.jesp.2011.01.001.

11. Bohns, Newark, and Xu, "For a dollar, would you . . . ?"

12. Francis J. Flynn, "How much is it worth to you? Subjective evaluations of help in organizations," *Research in Organizational Behavior* 27 (2006): 133–174, https://doi.org/10.1016/S0191-3085 (06)27004-7.

13. Francis J. Flynn, "What have you done for me lately? Temporal adjustments to favor evaluations," *Organizational Behavior and Human Decision Processes* 91, no. 1 (2003): 38–50, https://doi .org/10.1016/S0749-5978(02)00523-X.

14. *Dumbo*, directed by Ben Sharpsteen (Walt Disney Studios, 1941).

15. Flynn and Lake (Bohns), "If you need help, just ask."

16. Bohns, "(Mis)Understanding our influence over others."

17. Robert B. Cialdini, Betty Lee Darby, and Joyce E. Vincent, "Transgression and altruism: A case for hedonism," *Journal of Experimental Social Psychology* 9, no. 6 (1973): 502–516, https://doi.org/10 .1016/0022-1031(73)90031-0.

18. C. Daniel Batson, Judy G. Batson, Cari A. Griffitt, Sergio Barrientos, J. Randall Brandt, Peter Sprengelmeyer, and Michael J. Bayly, "Negative-state relief and the empathy—altruism hypothesis," *Journal of Personality and Social Psychology* 56, no. 6 (1989): 922, https://doi.org/10.1037/0022-3514.56.6.922.

19. Dale T. Miller, "The norm of self-interest," *American Psychologist* 54, no. 12 (1999): 1053, https://doi.org/10.1037/0003-066X.54.12 .1053.

20. Chip Heath, "On the social psychology of agency relationships: Lay theories of motivation overemphasize extrinsic incentives." *Organizational Behavior and Human Decision Processes* 78, no. 1 (1999): 25–62, https://doi.org/10.1006/obhd.1999.2826.

21. Daniel A. Newark, Vanessa K. Bohns, and Francis J. Flynn, "A

helping hand is hard at work: Help-seekers' underestimation of helpers' effort," *Organizational Behavior and Human Decision Processes* 139 (2017): 18–29, https://doi.org/10.1016/j.obhdp.2017 .01.001.

22. Flynn and Lake (Bohns), "If you need help, just ask."

23. Sharon Driscoll, "Paul Brest," *Stanford Lawyer* (2014). https://law .stanford.edu/stanford-lawyer/articles/paul-brest/.

24. Ibid.

25. Ibid.

26. Susan Bell, "Reflections upon a leader: Paul Brest, mentor and friend," *Stanford Law Review* (2000): 257–260, https://www.jstor .org/stable/1229479.

27. Paul Brest, "Fundraising, football and other lessons learned as dean," *Stanford Report* (1999). https://news.stanford.edu/news /1999/august25/brestvantage-825.html.

28. July 20, 2019, personal email correspondence.

CHAPTER 4: WHY IT'S SO HARD TO SAY "NO"

1. Erving Goffman, *The Presentation of Self in Everyday Life* (Anchor, 1959).

2. Sunita Sah, George Loewenstein, and Daylian Cain, "Insinuation anxiety: Concern that advice rejection will signal distrust after conflict of interest disclosures," *Personality and Social Psychology Bulletin* 45, no. 7 (2019): 1099–1112, https://doi.org/10 .1177/0146167218805991.

3. "Choking prevention and rescue tips," National Safety Council, https://www.nsc.org/home-safety/safety-topics/choking-suf focation.

4. Emma Hammett, "Have YOU ever choked on your food? The DIY guide to saving your own life . . . ," *Daily Mail*, January 27, 2017, https://www.dailymail.co.uk/health/article-4163960/Revealed -DIY-guide-not-dying-choking.html.

5. John Sabini, Michael Siepmann, and Julia Stein, "The really fundamental attribution error in social psychological research," *Psychological Inquiry* 12, no. 1 (2001): 1–15, https://doi.org/10.1207/ S15327965PLI1201_01.

6. John M. Darley and Bibb Latané, "Bystander intervention in emergencies: Diffusion of responsibility," *Journal of Personality and Social Psychology* 8, no. 4, p. 1 (1968): 377, https://doi.org/10.1037/h0025589.

7. Bibb Latané and John M. Darley, "Group inhibition of bystander intervention in emergencies," *Journal of Personality and Social Psychology* 10, no. 3 (1968): 215, https://doi.org/10.1037/h0026570.

8. Ibid.

9. Deborah A. Prentice and Dale T. Miller, "Pluralistic ignorance and the perpetuation of social norms by unwitting actors," in *Advances in Experimental Social Psychology*, vol. 28, 161–209 (Academic Press: 1996).

10. Bibb Latané and Judith Rodin, "A lady in distress: Inhibiting effects of friends and strangers on bystander intervention," *Journal of Experimental Social Psychology* 5, no. 2 (1969): 189–202, https://doi .org/10.1016/0022-1031(69)90046-8.

11. Sabini, Siepmann, and Stein, "The really fundamental attribution error."

12. Stanley Milgram, *Obedience to Authority: An Experimental View* (Harper & Row, 1974).

13. Thomas Blass, *Obedience to Authority: Current Perspectives on the Milgram Paradigm* (Lawrence Erlbaum Associates Publishers, 1999).

14. M. Mahdi Roghanizad and Vanessa K. Bohns, "Ask in person: You're less persuasive than you think over email," *Journal of Experimental Social Psychology*, 69 (2017): 223–226, https://doi .org/10.1016/j.jesp.2016.10.002.

15. Sabini, Siepmann, and Stein, "The really fundamental attribution error."

16. Leaf Van Boven, George Loewenstein, and David Dunning, "The illusion of courage in social predictions: Underestimating the impact of fear of embarrassment on other people," *Organizational Behavior and Human Decision Processes* 96, no. 2 (2005): 130–141, https://doi.org/10.1016/j.obhdp.2004.12.001.

17. Francis J. Flynn and Vanessa K. B. Lake (Bohns), "If you need help, just ask: Underestimating compliance with direct requests for help," *Journal of Personality and Social Psychology* 95, no. 1 (2008): 128, https://doi.org/10.1037/0022-3514.95.1.128.

18. Julie A. Woodzicka and Marianne LaFrance, "Real versus imagined gender harassment," *Journal of Social Issues* 57, no. 1 (2001): 15–30, https://doi.org/10.1111/0022-4537.00199.

19. Jennifer Randall Crosby and Johannes Wilson, "Let's not, and say we would: Imagined and actual responses to witnessing homophobia," *Journal of Homosexuality* 62, no. 7 (2015): 957–970, https://doi.org/10.1080/00918369.2015.1008284.

20. Kerry Kawakami, Elizabeth Dunn, Francine Karmali, and John F. Dovidio, "Mispredicting affective and behavioral responses to racism," *Science* 323, no. 5911 (2009): 276–278, https://doi.org/10.1126/science.1164951.

21. Kevin Mitnick, *Ghost in the Wires: My Adventures as the World's Most Wanted Hacker* (Little, Brown and Company, 2011).

22. Brad J. Sagarin and Kevin D. Mitnick, "The path of least resistance," in Douglas Kenrick, Noah Goldstein, and Sanford Braver, eds., *Six Degrees of Social Influence: Science, Application, and the Psychology of Robert Cialdini* (Oxford University Press: 2012).

23. "Alisa" and "Steve" from *Ghost in the Wires* are referred to as "Alice" and "John" in Sagarin and Mitnick's 2012 article.

24. Daryl J. Bem, "Self-perception theory," in *Advances in Experimental Social Psychology*, vol. 6, 1–62 (Academic Press, 1972), https://doi.org/10.1016/S0065-2601(08)60024-6.

CHAPTER 5: MISINFORMATION, INAPPROPRIATE ASKS, AND ME TOO

1. Gretchen Morgenson, "Debt watchdogs: Tamed or caught napping?," *New York Times*, December 6, 2008, https://www.nytimes.com/2008/12/07/business/07rating.html.

2. Vanessa K. Bohns, M. Mahdi Roghanizad, and Amy Z. Xu, "Underestimating our influence over others' unethical behavior and decisions," *Personality and Social Psychology Bulletin* 40, no. 3 (2014): 348–362, https://doi.org/10.1177/0146167213511825.

3. Vanessa K. Bohns, "(Mis)Understanding our influence over others: A review of the underestimation-of-compliance effect," *Current Directions in Psychological Science* 25, no. 2 (2016): 119–123, https://doi.org/10.1177/0963721415628011.

4. Bohns, Roghanizad, and Xu, "Underestimating our influence over others' unethical behavior."

5. Bohns, "(Mis)Understanding our influence over others."

6. Emma Brockes, "Me Too founder Tarana Burke: You have to use your privilege to serve other people," *The Guardian*, January 15, 2018, https://www.theguardian.com/world/2018/jan/15/me-too -founder-tarana-burke-women-sexual-assault.

7. Jodi Kantor and Megan Twohey, "Harvey Weinstein Paid Off Sexual Harassment Accusers for Decades," *New York Times*, October 5, 2017, https://www.nytimes.com/2017/10/05/us/harvey -weinstein-harassment-allegations.html.

8. Paul Farhi, "So, you had questions about that button on Matt Lauer's desk?," *Washington Post*, December 1, 2017, https://www .washingtonpost.com/lifestyle/style/so-you-had-questions-about -that-button-on-matt-lauers-desk/2017/12/01/48b1f7c2-d6bd-11e7 -a986-d0a9770d9a3e_story.html.

9. Louis C. K., "Louis C.K. responds to accusations: These stories are true," *New York Times,* November 10, 2017, https://www.nytimes .com/2017/11/10/arts/television/louis-ck-statement.html.

10. Anna North, "The Aziz Ansari story is ordinary, and that's why we have to talk about it," Vox, January 16, 2018, https://www.vox.com/ identities/2018/1/16/16894722/aziz-ansari-grace-babe-me-too.

11. Katie Way, "I went on a date with Aziz Ansari. It turned into the worst night of my life," Babe, https://babe.net/2018/01/13/aziz -ansari-28355.

12. Emily Stewart, "Aziz Ansari responds to sexual allegations against him," Vox, January 15, 2018, https://www.vox.com/ identities/2018/1/15/16893468/aziz-ansari-allegations.

13. Way, "I went on a date with Aziz Ansari."

14. Kelly McEvers and Caitlin Flanagan, "The fine line between a bad date and sexual assault: 2 views on Aziz Ansari," interviewed by Ari Shapiro, *All Things Considered*, NPR, January 16, 2018, https:// www.npr.org/2018/01/16/578422491/the-fine-line-between-a-bad -date-and-sexual-assault-two-views-on-aziz-ansari.

15. North, "The Aziz Ansari story is ordinary."

16. Kristen Roupenian, "Cat Person," *New Yorker*, December 4, 2017, https://www.newyorker.com/magazine/2017/12/11/cat-person.

17. Olga Khazan, "A viral short story for the #MeToo movement," *The Atlantic*, December 11, 2017, https://www.theatlantic.com/technology/archive/2017/12/a-viral-short-story-for-the-metoo-moment/548009/.

18. Roupenian, "Cat Person."

19. Megan Garber, "The weaponization of awkwardness," *The Atlantic*, December 15, 2017, https://www.theatlantic.com/entertainment/archive/2017/12/the-weaponization-of-awkwardness/548291/.

20. Ella Dawson, "'Bad sex,' or the sex we don't want but have anyway," *Elle*, December 12, 2017, https://www.elle.com/life-love/sex-relationships/a14414938/bad-sex-or-the-sex-we-dont-want-but-have-anyway/.

21. Emily A. Impett and Letitia A. Peplau, "Sexual compliance: Gender, motivational, and relationship perspectives," *Journal of Sex Research* 40, no. 1 (2003): 87–100, https://doi.org/10.1080/00224490309552169.

22. Garber, "The Weaponization of Awkwardness."

23. Samantha Joel, Rimma Teper, and Geoff MacDonald, "People overestimate their willingness to reject potential romantic partners by overlooking their concern for other people," *Psychological Science* 25, no. 12 (2014): 2233–2240, https://doi.org/10.1177/0956797614552828.

24. Vanessa K. Bohns and Lauren A. DeVincent, "Rejecting unwanted romantic advances is more difficult than suitors realize," *Social Psychological and Personality Science* 10, no. 8 (2019): 1102–1110, https://doi.org/10.1177/1948550618769880.

25. Louise F. Fitzgerald, Sandra L. Shullman, Nancy Bailey, Margaret Richards, Janice Swecker, Yael Gold, Mimi Omerod, and Lauren Weitzman, "The incidence and dimensions of sexual harassment in academia and the workplace," *Journal of Vocational Behavior* 32 (1988): 152–175, https://doi.org/10.1016/0001-8791(88)90012-7.

26. Reshma Jagsi, Kent A. Griffith, Rochelle Jones, Chithra R. Perumalswami, Peter Ubel, and Abigail Stewart, "Sexual harassment and discrimination experiences of academic medical faculty," *JAMA* 315, (2016): 2120–2121, https://doi.org/10.1001/jama.2016.2188.

27. Hope Jahren, "She wanted to do her research. He wanted to talk feelings," *New York Times*, March 4, 2016, https://www

.nytimes.com/2016/03/06/opinion/sunday/she-wanted-to-do-her
-research-he-wanted-to-talk-feelings.html.

28. Vanessa K. Bohns, "Why 'just go for it' is bad dating advice," *Character & Context*, February 20, 2020, http://www.spsp.org/news
-center/blog/bohns-unwanted-romantic-advances#gsc.tab=0.

29. Jada Yuan, "L.A. writer says Richard Dreyfuss sexually harassed
and exposed himself to her in the 1980's," Vulture, November
10, 2017, https://www.vulture.com/2017/11/richard-dreyfuss
-accused-of-exposing-himself-to-woman.html.

30. *Aziz Ansari: Right Now*, directed by Spike Jonze (Netflix, 2019).

31. Alain-Phillipe Durand, "Prepping for the campus visit," *Inside Higher Ed*, April 11, 2011, https://www.insidehighered.com/
advice/2011/04/11/prepping-campus-visit.

32. Lauren A. Rivera, *Pedigree: How Elite Students Get Elite Jobs* (Princeton University Press, 2016).

33. Lauren A. Rivera, "When two bodies are (not) a problem: Gender and relationship status discrimination in academic hiring," *American Sociological Review* 82, no. 6 (2017): 1111–1138, https://
doi.org/10.1177/0003122417739294.

34. Alexander H. Jordan and Emily M. Zitek, "Marital status bias in perceptions of employees," *Basic and Applied Social Psychology* 34, no. 5 (2012): 474–481, https://doi.org/10.1080/01973533.2012.711687.

35. Laura Davis, "You can't ask that! Unmasking the myths about 'illegal' pre-employment interview questions," *ALSB Journal of Employment and Labor Law* 12, 39–57, Spring 2011, https://castle
.eiu.edu/~alsb/Spring2011.html.

36. H. Gene Hern Jr., Tarak Trivedi, Harrison J. Alter, and Charlotte P. Wills, "How prevalent are potentially illegal questions during residency interviews? A follow-up study of applicants to all specialties in the National Resident Matching Program," *Academic Medicine* 91, no. 11 (2016): 1546–1553, https://doi.org/10.1097/ACM
.0000000000001181.

37. Vivian Giang, "11 common interview questions that are actually illegal," *Business Insider*, July 5, 2013, https://www.businessinsider
.com/11-illegal-interview-questions-2013-7.

38. Einav Hart, Eric VanEpps, and Maurice Schweitzer, "I didn't want to offend you: The cost of avoiding sensitive questions"

(working paper), Einav Hart, Eric M. VanEpps, and Maurice E. Schweitzer, "The (better than expected) consequences of asking sensitive questions," *Organizational Behavior and Human Decision Processes*, 162 (2021): 136–154, https://doi.org/10.1016/j .obhdp.2020.10.014.

39. Kathryn Greene, Valerian J. Derlega, and Alicia Mathews, "Self-disclosure in personal relationships," in A. L. Vangelisti and D. Perlman, eds., *The Cambridge Handbook of Personal Relationships* (Cambridge University Press, 2006): 409–427, https://doi.org/10 .1017/CBO9780511606632.023.

40. Catherine Shea, Sunita Sah, and Ashley Martin, "Just don't ask: Raising protected class issues in job interviews increases insinuation anxiety and negatively influences outcomes for employers and employees" (working paper).

41. Dolly Chugh, *The Person You Mean to Be: How Good People Fight Bias* (HarperCollins, 2018).

42. Harry G. Frankfurt, *On Bullshit* (Princeton University Press, 2005).

43. John V. Petrocelli, "Antecedents of bullshitting," *Journal of Experimental Social Psychology* 76 (2018): 249–258, https://doi.org/10 .1016/j.jesp.2018.03.004.

44. Gordon Pennycook and David G. Rand, "Who falls for fake news? The roles of bullshit receptivity, overclaiming, familiarity, and analytic thinking," *Journal of Personality* 88, no. 2 (2018): 185–200, https://doi.org/10.1111/jopy.12476.

45. Gordon Pennycook, James Allan Cheyne, Nathaniel Barr, Derek J. Koehler, and Jonathan A. Fugelsang, "On the reception and detection of pseudo-profound bullshit," *Judgment and Decision Making* 10, no. 6 (2015): 549–563, http://journal.sjdm.org/15/15923a/jdm15923a .html.

46. Soroush Vosoughi, Deb Roy, and Sinan Aral, "The spread of true and false news online," *Science* 359, no. 6380 (2018): 1146–1151, https://doi.org/10.1126/science.aap9559.

47. Gordan Pennycook and David G. Rand, "Lazy, not biased: Susceptibility to partisan fake news is better explained by lack of reasoning than by motivated reasoning," *Cognition* 188 (2019), 39–50, https://doi.org/10.1016/j.cognition.2018.06.011.

48. Michael S. Bernstein, Eytan Bakshy, Moira Burke, and Brian Karrer,

"Quantifying the invisible audience in social networks," *Proceedings of the SIGCHI Conference on Human Factors in Computing Systems* (2013): 21–30, https://doi.org/10.1145/2470654.2470658.

CHAPTER 6: POWER AND PERCEIVED INFLUENCE

1. Amy R. Wolfson and Mary A. Carskadon, "A survey of factors influencing high school start-times," *NASSP Bulletin* 89, no. 642 (2005): 47–66, https://doi.org/10.1177/019263650508964205.
2. Mary A. Carskadon, Susan E. Labyak, Christine Acebo, and Ronald Seifer, "Intrinsic circadian period of adolescent humans measured in conditions of forced desynchrony," *Neuroscience Letters* 260, no. 2 (1999): 129–132, https://doi.org/10.1016/S0304-3940(98)00971-9.
3. Jere Longman, "College Basketball East: Once lowly, Sankes and Holy Cross bounce back," March 15, 2001, *New York Times,* https://www.nytimes.com/2001/03/15/sports/college-basketball-east-once-lowly-sankes-and-holy-cross-bounce-back.html.
4. John Feinstein, *The Last Amateurs: Playing for Glory and Honor in Division I College Basketball* (Back Bay Books, 2008).
5. Ibid.
6. Ibid.
7. Longman, "College Basketball East."
8. "Jocks can sue over nude drill as court strips earlier decision," July 1, 2001, *New Brunswick Daily Herald,* https://www.heraldextra.com/sports/jocks-can-sue-over-nude-drill-as-court-strips-earlier/article_8916f968-d533-55ce-a052-a985989843c9.html.
9. Longman, "College Basketball East."
10. Ibid.
11. Welch Suggs, "N.J. court allows Rutgers athletes to sue over being forced to run naked," *Chronicle of Higher Education,* https://www.chronicle.com/article/NJ-Court-Allows-Rutgers/9622.
12. Ken Davis, "Bannon's actions get under Rutgers' skin," *Hartford Courant,* September 12, 1999, https://www.courant.com/news/connecticut/hc-xpm-1999-09-12-9909120266-story.html.
13. Feinstein, *The Last Amateurs.*
14. Ibid.
15. Susan T. Fiske, "Controlling other people: The impact of power on

stereotyping," *American Psychologist* 48, no. 6 (1993): 621, https://doi.org/10.1037/0003-066X.48.6.621.

16. Adam D. Galinsky, Joe C. Magee, M. Ena Inesi, and Deborah H. Gruenfeld, "Power and perspectives not taken," *Psychological Science* 17, no. 12 (2006): 1068–1074, https://doi.org/10.1111/j.1467-9280.2006.01824.x.

17. Adam D. Galinsky, Derek D. Rucker, and Joe C. Magee, "Power and perspective-taking: A critical examination," *Journal of Experimental Social Psychology* 67 (2016): 91–92, https://doi.org/10.1016/j.jesp.2015.12.002.

18. Marianne Schmid Mast, Klaus Jonas, and Judith A. Hall, "Give a person power and he or she will show interpersonal sensitivity: The phenomenon and its why and when," *Journal of Personality and Social Psychology* 97, no. 5 (2009): 835, https://doi.org/10.1037/a0016234.

19. Galinsky, Rucker, and Magee, "Power and perspective-taking."

20. Adam D. Galinsky, Joe C. Magee, Deborah H. Gruenfeld, Jennifer A. Whitson, and Katie A. Liljenquist, "Power reduces the press of the situation: implications for creativity, conformity, and dissonance," *Journal of Personality and Social Psychology,* 95, no. 6 (2008): 1450, https://doi.org/10.1037/a0012633.

21. Adam D. Galinsky, Deborah H. Gruenfeld, and Joe C. Magee, "From power to action," *Journal of Personality and Social Psychology* 85, no. 3 (2003): 453, https://doi.org/10.1037/0022-3514.85.3.453.

22. Yidan Yin, Krishna Savani, and Pamela Smith, "From power to choice: A high sense of power increases blame" (working paper).

23. Adam Galinsky, "When you're in charge, your whisper may feel like a shout," *New York Times*, August 15, 2015, https://www.nytimes.com/2015/08/16/jobs/when-youre-in-charge-your-whisper-may-feel-like-a-shout.html.

24. *The Devil Wears Prada*, directed by David Frankel (20th Century Fox, 2006).

25. Heather Caygle, John Bresnahan, and Kyle Cheney, "Rep. Katie Hill to resign amid allegations of inappropriate relationships with staffers," *Politico*, October 27, 2019, https://www.politico.com/news/2019/10/27/rep-katie-hill-to-resign-amid-allegations-of-inappropriate-relationships-with-staffers-000301.

26. Yusaf Khan, "McDonald's loses $4 billion in value after CEO fired

over relationship with subordinate," *Business Insider,* November 4, 2019, https://markets.businessinsider.com/news/stocks/mcdonalds-stock-price-billions-wiped-from-value-on-fired-ceo-easterbrook-2019-11-1028654817.

27. Danielle Wiener-Bronner, "McDonald's CEO Steve Easterbrook is out for 'consensual relationship with an employee,'" CNN.com, November 4, 2019, https://www.cnn.com/2019/11/03/business/mcdonalds-ceo-steve-easterbrook-steps-down/index.html.

28. Paula McDonald, "Banning workplace romances won't solve the problem of sexual misconduct in the workplace," *The Conversation,* February 15, 2018, https://theconversation.com/banning-workplace-romances-wont-solve-the-problem-of-sexual-misconduct-in-the-office-91975

29. "President endorses consensual relationship policy," *Cornell Chronicle,* May 21, 2018, https://news.cornell.edu/stories/2018/05/president-endorses-consensual-relationship-policy.

30. Hope Jahren, "She wanted to do her research. He wanted to talk feelings," *New York Times,* March 4, 2016, https://www.nytimes.com/2016/03/06/opinion/sunday/she-wanted-to-do-her-research-he-wanted-to-talk-feelings.html.

31. Elizabeth Wagmeister, "Matt Lauer accuser Brook Nevils slams him for victim blaming," *Variety,* October 10, 2019, https://variety.com/2019/tv/news/matt-lauer-accuser-victim-blaming-1203365926/.

32. Ronan Farrow, "From aggressive overtures to sexual assault: Harvey Weinstein's accusers tell their stories," *New Yorker,* October 10, 2017, https://www.newyorker.com/news/news-desk/from-aggressive-overtures-to-sexual-assault-harvey-weinsteins-accusers-tell-their-stories.

33. Dilvan Yasa, "There can be no winners: The consequences of sleeping with my boss," *Syndey Herald,* December 9, 2017, https://www.smh.com.au/lifestyle/life-and-relationships/i-came-out-realising-there-can-be-no-winners-the-consequences-of-sleeping-with-my-boss-20171207-h00g47.html.

34. Monica Lewinsky, "Shame and survival," *Vanity Fair,* May 6, 2014, https://www.vanityfair.com/news/2014/05/monica-lewinsky-speaks.

35. "Public shaming," *Last Week Tonight with John Oliver*, March 18, 2019, HBO.
36. Vanessa K. Bohns, "McDonald's fired its CEO for sleeping with an employee—research shows why even consensual office romances can be a problem," *The Conversation*, November 1, 2019, https://the conversation.com/mcdonalds-fired-its-ceo-for-sleeping-with-an -employee-research-shows-why-even-consensual-office-romances -can-be-a-problem-126231.
37. Antonia Abbey, "Sex differences in attributions for friendly behavior: Do males misperceive females' friendliness?," *Journal of Personality and Social Psychology* 42, no. 5 (1982): 830, https://doi .org/10.1037/0022-3514.42.5.830.
38. John A. Bargh, Paula Raymond, John B. Pryor, and Fritz Strack, "Attractiveness of the underling: An automatic power → sex asso- ciation and its consequences for sexual harassment and aggres- sion," *Journal of Personality and Social Psychology* 68, no. 5 (1995): 768, https://doi.org/10.1037/0022-3514.68.5.768.
39. Monica Lewinsky, "Emerging from the 'house of gaslight' in the age of #metoo," *Vanity Fair*, March 2018, https://www.vanityfair .com/news/2018/02/monica-lewinsky-in-the-age-of-metoo.
40. Sarah Maslin Nir, "How 2 lives clashed in Central Park, rattling the nation," *New York Times*, June 14, 2020, https://www.nytimes .com/2020/06/14/nyregion/central-park-amy-cooper-christian -racism.html.
41. Evan Hill, Ainara Tiefenthäler, Christiaan Triebert, Drew Jordan, Haley Willis, and Robin Stein, "How George Floyd was killed in police custody," *New York Times*, Jun 22, 2020, https://www .nytimes.com/2020/05/31/us/george-floyd-investigation.html.
42. Ginia Bellafante, "Why Amy Cooper's use of 'African American' stung," *New York Times*, May 29, 2020, https://www.nytimes .com/2020/05/29/nyregion/Amy-Cooper-Central-Park-racism .html.
43. Frank Edwards, Hedwig Lee, and Michael Esposito, "Risk of being killed by police use of force in the United States by age, race- ethnicity, and sex," *Proceedings of the National Academy of Sciences* 116, no. 34 (2019): 16793–16798, https://doi.org/10.1073/pnas .1821204116.

44. Shane Goldmacher, "Racial justice groups flooded with millions in donations in wake of Floyd death," *New York Times,* June 14, 2020, https://www.nytimes.com/2020/06/14/us/politics/black-lives-matter-racism-donations.html.

45. Philip Marcel, "Black-owned businesses see sales surge amid racism reckoning," Associated Press, July 1, 2020, https://apnews.com/5738fc904a6b29118e63a5d762f48791.

46. Marguerite Ward, "The NYT bestseller list this week is almost entirely comprised of books about race and white privilege in America," *Business Insider*, June 11, 2020, https://www.businessinsider.com/new-york-times-bestseller-list-books-about-race-in-america-2020-6.

47. Dionne Searcey and David Zucchino, "Protests swell across America as George Floyd is mourned near his birthplace," *New York Times,* June 6, 2020, https://www.nytimes.com/2020/06/06/us/protests-today-police-george-floyd.html.

48. Soledad O'Brien, "A MeToo movement for journalists of color," *New York Times,* July 4, 2020, https://www.nytimes.com/2020/07/04/opinion/soledad-obrien-racism-journalism.html?action=click&module=Opinion&pgtype=Homepage.

49. Kerry Flynn, "Refinery29 is reeling from claims of racism and toxic work culture. Employees say it's even worse behind the scenes," CNN.com, June 11, 2020, https://www.cnn.com/2020/06/11/media/refinery29-workplace-culture/index.html.

50. Concepción de León and Elizabeth A. Harris, "#PublishingPaidMe and a Day of Action Reveal an Industry Reckoning," *New York Times,* June 8, 2020, https://www.nytimes.com/2020/06/08/books/publishingpaidme-publishing-day-of-action.html.

51. Mary Louise Kelly, "#PublishingPaidMe: Authors share their advances to expose racial disparaties," *All Things Considered*, NPR, June 8, 2020, https://www.npr.org/2020/06/08/872470156/-publishingpaidme-authors-share-their-advances-to-expose-racial-disparities.

52. Nidhi Subbaraman, "How #BlackInTheIvory put a spotlight on racism in academia," *Nature*, June 11, 2020, https://www.nature.com/articles/d41586-020-01741-7.

53. Neil Lewis, "What I've learned about being a Black scientist,"

Science, June 16, 2020, https://www.sciencemag.org/careers/2020/06/what-ive-learned-about-being-black-scientist.

54. Karen E. Fields and Barbara Jeanne Fields, *Racecraft: The Soul of Inequality in American Life* (Verso Trade, 2014).

55. Ibram X. Kendi, *Stamped from the Beginning: The Definitive History of Racist Ideas in America* (Random House, 2017).

56. Bruce Western and Becky Pettit, "Black-white wage inequality, employment rates, and incarceration," *American Journal of Sociology* 111, no. 2 (2005): 553–578, https://doi.org/10.1086/432780.

57. Zinzi D. Bailey, Nancy Krieger, Madina Agénor, Jasmine Graves, Natalia Linos, and Mary T. Bassett, "Structural racism and health inequities in the USA: evidence and interventions," *The Lancet* 389, no. 10077 (2017): 1453–1463, https://doi.org/10.1016/S0140-6736(17)30569-X.

58. Becky Pettit and Bruce Western, "Mass imprisonment and the life course: Race and class inequality in US incarceration," *American Sociological Review* 69, no. 2 (2004): 151–169, https://doi.org/10.1177/000312240406900201.

59. Edwards, Lee, and Esposito, "Risk of being killed by police."

60. Sean F. Reardon, "School segregation and racial academic achievement gaps," *RSF: The Russell Sage Foundation Journal of the Social Sciences* 2, no. 5 (2016): 34–57, https://www.rsfjournal.org/content/2/5/34.short.

61. Ted Thornhill, "We want black students, just not you: How white admissions counselors screen black prospective students," *Sociology of Race and Ethnicity* 5, no. 4 (2019): 456–470, https://doi.org/10.1177/2332649218792579.

62. Marianne Bertrand and Sendhil Mullainathan, "Are Emily and Greg more employable than Lakisha and Jamal? A field experiment on labor market discrimination," *American Economic Review* 94, no. 4 (2004): 991–1013, https://doi.org/10.3386/w9873.

63. Gregory Smithsimon, "How to see race," Aeon, March 26, 2018, https://aeon.co/essays/race-is-not-real-what-you-see-is-a-power-relationship-made-flesh.

64. Nell Irvin Painter, "Why 'White' should be capitalized, too," *Washington Post*, July 22, 2020.

65. Jennifer L. Eberhardt, *Biased: Uncovering the Hidden Prejudice that Shapes What We See, Think, and Do* (Penguin Books, 2020).

66. Victoria C. Plaut, Kecia M. Thomas, and Matt J. Goren, "Is multiculturalism or color blindness better for minorities?," *Psychological Science* 20, no. 4 (2009): 444–446, https://doi.org/10.1111/j.1467-9280.2009.02318.x.

67. Sonia K. Kang, Katherine A. DeCelles, András Tilcsik, and Sora Jun, "Whitened résumés: Race and self-presentation in the labor market," *Administrative Science Quarterly* 61, no. 3 (2016): 469-502, https://doi.org/10.1177/0001839216639577.

68. Courtney L. McCluney, Robotham, Kathrina, Lee, Serenity, Smith, Richard, and Durkee, Miles, "The costs of code-switching," *Harvard Business Review,* November 15, 2019, https://hbr.org/2019/11/the-costs-of-codeswitching.

69. Elijah Anderson, "The white space," *Sociology of Race and Ethnicity* 1, no. 1 (2015): 10–21, https://doi.org/10.1177/2332649214561306.

70. Ibid.

71. Fiske, "Controlling other people: The impact of power on stereotyping."

72. John Biewen and Chenjerai Kumanyika, "Seeing white: Episode 6: That's not us, so we're clean," Scene on Radio Season 2, Center for Documentary Studies, Distributed by PRX, http://www.sceneonradio.org/tag/season-2/.

73. Ramesh Nagarajah, "Reflections from a token black friend," Medium, June 4, 2020, https://humanparts.medium.com/reflections-from-a-token-black-friend-2f1ea522d42d.

74. Chana Joffe-Walt, "Episode 1: The book of statuses," *Nice White Parents* podcast, July 30, 2020.

75. Naomi Tweyo Nkinsi, Twitter status, June 13, 2020, https://twitter.com/NNkinsi/status/1271855868531765253.

76. Derald Wing Sue, Christina M. Capodilupo, Gina C. Torino, Jennifer M. Bucceri, Aisha Holder, Kevin L. Nadal, and Marta Esquilin, "Racial microaggressions in everyday life: implications for clinical practice," *American Psychologist* 62, no. 4 (2007): 271, https://doi.org/10.1037/0003-066X.62.4.271.

77. Courtney L. McCluney, Lauren L. Schmitz, Margaret T. Hicken, and Amanda Sonnega, "Structural racism in the workplace: Does perception matter for health inequalities?," *Social Science &*

Medicine 199 (2018): 106–114, https://doi.org/10.1016/j.socscimed.2017.05.039.

78. Arline T. Geronimus, Margaret Hicken, Danya Keene, and John Bound, "'Weathering' and age patterns of allostatic load scores among blacks and whites in the United States," *American Journal of Public Health* 96, no. 5 (2006): 826–833, https://doi.org/10.2105/AJPH.2004.060749.

79. Arthur W. Blume, Laura V. Lovato, Bryan N. Thyken, and Natasha Denny, "The relationship of microaggressions with alcohol use and anxiety among ethnic minority college students in a historically white institution," *Cultural Diversity and Ethnic Minority Psychology* 18, no. 1 (2012): 45, https://doi.org/10.1037/a0025457.

80. Oscar Holmes IV, Kaifeng Jiang, Derek R. Avery, Patrick F. McKay, In-Sue Oh, and C. Justice Tillman, "A meta-analysis integrating 25 years of diversity climate research," *Journal of Management* (2020), https://doi.org/10.1177/0149206320934547.

81. Andrew R. Todd and Adam D. Galinsky, "Perspective-taking as a strategy for improving intergroup relations: Evidence, mechanisms, and qualifications," *Social and Personality Psychology Compass* 8, no. 7 (2014): 374–387, https://doi.org/10.1111/spc3.12116.

82. Tal Eyal, Mary Steffel, and Nicholas Epley, "Perspective mistaking: Accurately understanding the mind of another requires getting perspective, not taking perspective," *Journal of Personality and Social Psychology* 114, no. 4 (2018): 547, https://doi.org/10.1037/pspa0000115.

83. Jeff Moag, "The power of inclusion," May 7, 2020, https://www.tuck.dartmouth.edu/news/articles/the-power-of-inclusion.

84. Teresa Amabile, Colin Fisher, and Julianna Pillemer, "Ideo's culture of helping," *Harvard Business Review*, January–February 2014, https://hbr.org/2014/01/ideos-culture-of-helping.

85. Whitelaw Reid, "Reddit co-founder Alexis Ohanian says it was long past time to do the right thing," *UVA Today*, June 23, 2020, https://news.virginia.edu/content/reddit-co-founder-alexis-ohanian-says-it-was-long-past-time-do-right-thing.

86. "Address of President-Elect John F. Kennedy Delivered to a Joint Convention of the General Court of the Commonwealth of Massachusetts," January 9, 1961, https://www.jfklibrary.org/archives/other-resources/john-f-kennedy-speeches/massachusetts-general-court-19610109.

87. Kai Sassenberg, Naomi Ellemers, Daan Scheepers, and Annika Scholl, "'Power corrupts' revisited: The role of construal of power as opportunity or responsibility," in J.-W. van Prooijen and Paul A. M. van Lange, ed., *Power, Politics, and Paranoia: Why People Are Suspicious of Their Leaders* (2014): 73–87, https://doi.org/10.1017/CBO9781139565417.007.

88. Annika Scholl, Frank de Wit, Naomi Ellemers, Adam K. Fetterman, Kai Sassenberg, and Daan Scheepers, "The burden of power: Construing power as responsibility (rather than as opportunity) alters threat-challenge responses," *Personality and Social Psychology Bulletin* 44, no. 7 (2018): 1024–1038, https://doi.org/10.1177/0146167218757452.

89. Kai Sassenberg, Naomi Ellemers, and Daan Scheepers, "The attraction of social power: The influence of construing power as opportunity versus responsibility," *Journal of Experimental Social Psychology* 48, no. 2 (2012): 550–555, https://doi.org/10.1016/j.jesp.2011.11.008.

90. Serena Chen, Annette Y. Lee-Chai, and John A. Bargh, "Relationship orientation as a moderator of the effects of social power," *Journal of Personality and Social Psychology* 80, no. 2 (2001): 173, https://doi.org/10.1037/0022-3514.80.2.173.

91. Schmid Mast, Jonas, and Hall, "Give a person power."

92. Bob Gilber, "More than just a game," *Seton Hall Magazine,* November 9, 2010, https://blogs.shu.edu/magazine/2010/11/more-than-just-a-game-2/.

93. Longman, "College Basketball East."

CHAPTER 7: SEEING, FEELING, AND EXPERIENCING YOUR INFLUENCE OVER OTHERS

1. Patricia Mazzei and Frances Robles, "The costly toll of not shutting down spring break earlier," *New York Times,* April 11, 2020, https://www.nytimes.com/2020/04/11/us/florida-spring-break-coronavirus.html.

2. Jake Wittich, "St. Patrick's Day partiers hit the town over officials' pleas amid coronavirus outbreak," *Chicago Sun-Times,* March 14, 2020, https://chicago.suntimes.com/coronavirus/2020/3/14/21179885/st-patricks-day-chicago-coronavirus.

3. Taylor Lorenz, "Flight of the influencers," *New York Times,* April 3, 2020, https://www.nytimes.com/2020/04/02/style/influencers -leave-new-york-coronavirus.html?fbclid=IwAR3xnN5uIgtlZh5F bB09eik5htn3DYH9DwbRMFL4y_zPugpcgf2hZPyhkNo.

4. Vanessa K. Bohns, "Why so many people are still going out and congregating in groups despite coronavirus pandemic: It's not self-ishness," *The Hill,* March 20, 2020, https://thehill.com/changing -america/opinion/488654-why-so-many-people-are-still-going -out-and-congregating-in-groups.

5. Dale T. Miller, "The norm of self-interest," *American Psychologist 54,* no. 12 (1999): 1053–1060, https://doi.org/10.1037/0003-066X .54.12.1053.

6. Aimee Ortiz, "Man who said, 'If I get corona, I get corona,' apol-ogizes," *New York Times,* March 24, 2020, https://www.nytimes .com/2020/03/24/us/coronavirus-brady-sluder-spring-break.html.

7. Rachel Greenspan, "In a tearful post from the Hamptons, an influencer apologized after fleeing NYC following her COVID-19 diagnosis," *Insider,* April 2, 2020, https://www.insider.com/arielle -charnas-something-navy-responds-to-backlash-coronavirus -2020-4.

8. Caitlin O'Kane, "Woman helped elderly couple get food when they were too scared to go shopping during coronavirus outbreak," CBS News, March 13, 2020, https://www.cbsnews.com/news/ coronavirus-elderly-rebecca-mehra-twitter-buys-couple-groceries -scared-to-go-into-store-during-oregon-outbreak/.

9. "8-year-old NC child with autism gets surprise 100+ Jeep parade for birthday," *North Carolina News,* CBS17.com, https://www .cbs17.com/news/north-carolina-news/8-year-old-nc-child-with -autism-gets-surprise-100-jeep-parade-for-birthday/.

10. Max H. Bazerman, George Loewenstein, and Don A. Moore, "Why good accountants do bad audits," *Harvard Business Review* 80, no. 11 (2002): 96–103, https://hbr.org/2002/11/why-good -accountants-do-bad-audits.

11. Georgia Nigro and Ulric Neisser, "Point of view in personal mem-ories," *Cognitive Psychology* 15, no. 4 (1983): 467–482, https://doi .org/10.1016/0010-0285(83)90016-6.

12. Daniel T. Gilbert and Edward E. Jones, "Perceiver-induced con-straint: Interpretations of self-generated reality," *Journal of*

Personality and Social Psychology 50, no. 2 (1986): 269, https://doi
.org/10.1037/0022-3514.50.2.269.

13. Lisa K. Libby and Richard P. Eibach,"Visual perspective in mental imagery: A representational tool that functions in judgment, emotion, and self-insight," in J. M. Olson and M. P. Zanna, ed., *Advances in Experimental Social Psychology, vol. 44* (Academic Press, 2011): 185–245, https://doi.org/10.1016/B978-0-12-385522-0.00004-4.

14. Lisa K. Libby, Eric M. Shaeffer, Richard P. Eibach, and Jonathan A. Slemmer, "Picture yourself at the polls: Visual perspective in mental imagery affects self-perception and behavior," *Psychological Science* 18, no. 3 (2007): 199–203, https://doi.org/10.1111/j.1467-9280.2007.01872.x.

15. Ibid.

16. Eli J. Finkel, Erica B. Slotter, Laura B. Luchies, Gregory M. Walton, and James J. Gross, "A brief intervention to promote conflict reappraisal preserves marital quality over time," *Psychological Science* 24, no. 8 (2013): 1595–1601, https://doi.org/10.1177/0956797612474938.

17. Rebecca D. Ray, Frank H. Wilhelm, and James J. Gross, "All in the mind's eye? Anger rumination and reappraisal," *Journal of Personality and Social Psychology* 94, no. 1 (2008): 133, https://doi.org/10.1037/0022-3514.94.1.133.

18. Ethan Kross, Ozlem Ayduk, and Walter Mischel, "When asking 'why' does not hurt distinguishing rumination from reflective processing of negative emotions," *Psychological Science* 16, no. 9 (2005): 709–715, https://doi.org/10.1111/j.1467-9280.2005.01600.x.

19. Dale Carnegie, *How to Win Friends and Influence People* (Simon & Schuster, 1936).

20. Nicholas Epley, *Mindwise: Why We Misunderstand What Others Think, Believe, Feel, and Want* (Vintage, 2014).

21. Tal Eyal, Mary Steffel, and Nicholas Epley, "Perspective mistaking: Accurately understanding the mind of another requires getting perspective, not taking perspective," *Journal of Personality and Social Psychology* 114, no. 4 (2018): 547, https://doi.org/10.1037/pspa0000115.

22. C. Daniel Batson, Shannon Early, and Giovanni Salvarani,

"Perspective taking: Imagining how another feels versus imaging how you would feel," *Personality and Social Psychology Bulletin* 23, no. 7 (1997): 751–758, https://doi.org/10.1177/0146167297237008.

23. Adam D. Galinsky, Gillian Ku, and Cynthia S. Wang, "Perspective-taking and self-other overlap: Fostering social bonds and facilitating social coordination," *Group Processes & Intergroup Relations* 8, no. 2 (2005): 109–124, https://doi.org/10.1177/1368430205051060.

24. Andrew R. Todd, Galen V. Bodenhausen, Jennifer A. Richeson, and Adam D. Galinsky, "Perspective taking combats automatic expressions of racial bias," *Journal of Personality and Social Psychology* 100, no. 6 (2011): 1027, https://doi.org/10.1037/a0022308.

25. Eyal, Steffel, and Epley, "Perspective mistaking," 568.

26. Vanessa K. Bohns and Lauren A. DeVincent, "Rejecting unwanted romantic advances is more difficult than suitors realize," *Social Psychological and Personality Science* 10, no. 8 (2019): 1102–1110, https://doi.org/10.1177/1948550618769880.

27. Rachel L. Ruttan, Mary-Hunter McDonnell, and Loran F. Nordgren, "Having 'been there' doesn't mean I care: When prior experience reduces compassion for emotional distress," *Journal of Personality and Social Psychology* 108, no. 4 (2015): 610, https://doi.org/10.1037/pspi0000012.

28. Lee Ross, David Greene, and Pamela House, "The 'false consensus effect': An egocentric bias in social perception and attribution processes," *Journal of Experimental Social Psychology* 13, no. 3 (1977): 279–301, https://doi.org/10.1016/0022-1031(77)90049-X.

29. Alix Spiegel, "By making a game out of rejection, a man conquers fear," *Invisibilia*, NPR, January 16, 2015, https://www.npr.org/sections/health-shots/2015/01/16/377239011/by-making-a-game-out-of-rejection-a-man-conquers-fear.

30. Jonathan S. Abramowitz, Brett J. Deacon, and Stephen PH Whiteside, *Exposure Therapy for Anxiety: Principles and Practice* (Guilford Publications, 2019).

31. Jia Jiang, "Day 7: Speak over Costco's intercom," 100 Days of Rejection Therapy, *Rejection Therapy with Jian Jiang*, November 22, 2012, https://www.rejectiontherapy.com/blog/2012/11/22/day-7-rejection-therapy-speak-over-costcos-intercom/.

32. Jia Jiang, "Day 9: Send stuff to Santa Claus through FedEx,"

100 Days of Rejection Therapy, *Rejection Therapy with Jian Jiang*, November 24, 2012, https://www.rejectiontherapy.com/blog/2012/11/24/day-9-rejection-therapy-send-stuff-to-santa-claus-through-fedex/.

33. Jia Jiang, "Day 36: Trim my hair at PetSmart," 100 Days of Rejection Therapy, *Rejection Therapy with Jian Jiang*, January 4, 2013, https://www.rejectiontherapy.com/blog/2013/01/04/day-36-trim-my-hair-at-petsmart/.

34. Jia Jiang, "Day 41: Sit in police car's driver's seat," 100 Days of Rejection Therapy, *Rejection Therapy with Jian Jiang*, January 12, 2013, https://www.rejectiontherapy.com/blog/2013/01/12/rejection-41-sit-in-police-cars-drivers-seat/.

35. Jia Jiang, "Day 21: Ask strangers for compliments," 100 Days of Rejection Therapy, *Rejection Therapy with Jian Jiang*, December 9, 2012, https://www.rejectiontherapy.com/blog/2012/12/09/day-21-ask-strangers-for-compliments/.

36. Jia Jang, "Day 3: Ask for Olympic symbol donuts," 100 Days of Rejection Therapy, November 18, 2012, https://www.rejectiontherapy.com/blog/2012/11/18/day-3-rejection-therapy-ask-for-olympic-symbol-doughnuts-jackie-delivers/.

37. Jia Jiang, "What I learned from 100 days of rejection," TEDxMt-Hood, May 2015, https://www.ted.com/talks/jia_jiang_what_i_learned_from_100_days_of_rejection.

38. Steven O. Roberts, Carmelle Bareket-Shavit, Forrest A. Dollins, Peter D. Goldie, and Elizabeth Mortenson, "Racial inequality in psychological research: Trends of the past and recommendations for the future," *Perspectives on Psychological Science* (2020), https://doi.org/10.1177/1745691620927709.

39. Linda Babcock and Sara Laschever, *Women Don't Ask: Negotiation and the Gender Divide* (Princeton University Press, 2009).

40. "Hayley: Asking for Rejection," *My Name Is . . .* , BBC Radio 4, February 19, 2020, https://www.bbc.co.uk/programmes/m000ffzx.

41. Jiang, "Day 21: Ask strangers for compliments," 100 Days of Rejection Therapy (video).

42. Marianne Power, "I was rejected every day for a month," *Bazaar*, January 30, 2019, https://www.harpersbazaar.com/culture/features/a26062963/what-is-rejection-therapy-self-help/.

43. Vanessa K. Bohns, "(Mis)Understanding our influence over others: A review of the underestimation-of-compliance effect," *Current Directions in Psychological Science* 25, no. 2 (2016): 119–123, https://doi.org/10.1177/0963721415628011.

44. Paul Rozin and Edward B. Royzman, "Negativity bias, negativity dominance, and contagion," *Personality and Social Psychology Review* 5, no. 4 (2001): 296–320, https://doi.org/10.1207/S15327957PSPR0504_2.

45. Roy F. Baumeister, Ellen Bratslavsky, Catrin Finkenauer, and Kathleen D. Vohs, "Bad is stronger than good," *Review of General Psychology* 5, no. 4 (2001): 323–370, https://doi.org/10.1037/1089-2680.5.4.323.

46. Arielle M. Silverman, Jason D. Gwinn, and Leaf Van Boven, "Stumbling in their shoes: Disability simulations reduce judged capabilities of disabled people," *Social Psychological and Personality Science* 6, no. 4 (2015): 464–471, https://doi.org/10.1177/1948550614559650.

47. Jiang, TEDx Talk.

Index

actions, indirect effects of, 25–26
advances
    rejection of, 175–76
    saying "no" to, 105–12
    unwanted, 105–12, 175–76, 184
agreement, inclination toward,
    42–46
Ansari, Aziz, 104–5, 111, 177
appeasement, 91
Aral, Sinan, 120
Argento, Asia, 139
Atlantic, 106
attendance, importance of,
    26–27
attention
    getting, 2–3
    paid, 6–9, 26
audience, harnessing power of
    being in the, 14–22
"audience tuning," 17–22, 20–21

Babcock, Linda, 182
Bae, Sangah, 33
Bannon, Kevin, 129–31, 136–37

Barbash, Fred, 3–4
Bargh, John, 4–5, 9–10, 11–13
"behavioral contagion," 23–26
Bem, Daryl, 97
Bernstein, Michael, 122
biases, becoming aware of,
    160–61
Black Americans, indignities suf-
    fered by, 144–46
#BlackintheIvory, 145, 150
Boothby, Erica, ix–x, 4–5, 6,
    9–10, 11–13, 35–36
Brest, Paul, 70–71, 73
Britt, Anne, 40–41
Brown, Peter, 22–23, 26
"bullshitting," 118
bullying, 176
Burke, Tarana, 103
"bystander effect," 77

calmness, advantages of, 46–51
Carnegie, Dale, 170
Carskadon, Mary, 125–28
"Cat Person," 105, 106

Chauvin, Derek, 144
choice, power and, 131–37
Chugh, Dolly, 117
Cialdini, Robert, 37–38, 40
circadian rhythms, study of, 125–28
Clark, Margaret, 4–5, 9–10, 11–13, 35–36
Clinton, Bill, 140–41
Clinton, Hillary, 17, 22
Cobb, Ty, 3, 4
"code-switching," 148
coercion, sexual, 139–42
"cognitive misers," 38–39
"colorblindness," 148
Colvin, Alex, 71–72
Comely, Jason, 178–79, 180, 181, 185
"coming to the table," 26–27
communication, as cooperative endeavor, 42–46
comparison, 29–31
compliance, 105–12
  reasons for, 60, 66–67
complimenting strangers, x–xii, xiii
conversations, anxiety about, 34–38, 34–42
Cooney, Gus, 35–36
Cooper, Amy, 144
Cooper, Christian, 144
copying, 22–26
Countrywide Financial, 100
COVID-19 crisis, 157–58
credit rating agencies, 99–100
Crockett, Molly, 38
Crosby, Jennifer, 91

Darley, John, 77, 134–35
Davidai, Shai, 29–31
Davis, Shardé, 145
Dawson, Ella, 106
deference, misreading of, 143
Deri, Sebastian, 29–31, 33
desire to be helpful, 96–97, 158–59, 179–80
DeVincent, Lauren, 108, 174–75
"diffusion of responsibility," 78–80, 82
disclosure, 112–17
discrimination, 91–92
diversity, 150–51
"Donald study," 20–21
Dowd, John, 3, 4
Dowling, Sara, 159–60
Dreyfuss, Richard, 111
Dunning, David, 86

Easterbrook, Steve, 137, 141
Eberhardt, Jennifer, 148
embarrassment
  abuse of power of, 93–95
  fear of, 76–81, 93–95, 96, 134–35
  minimization of importance/ power of, 84–89
Epley, Nicholas, xi–xii, 170
exemplars, 29–31
experiential interventions. See also specific interventions
  power of, 188–89
  problems with, 186–87
exposure therapy, 179
Eyal, Tal, 170, 173, 174
eye contact, 5–6

"face," 86, 92
"facework," 76
Farrow, Ronan, 139
Feinstein, John, 129, 130
Finkel, Eli, 167–68
Floyd, George, 144, 149
Flynn, Frank, 53–54, 55, 61–64, 66, 68, 87–88
Frank, Robert, 24
Frankfurt, Harry, 118
Franklin, Marina, 16
friendliness, misinterpreted as romantic interest, 142–43
"fuzzy-trace theory," 41

Gadsby, Hannah, 16
Galinsky, Adam, 131–34, 136
Garber, Megan, 106
"gaze deflection," 5–6
gender, Rejection Therapy and, 182–84
getting into others' heads, 169–78
getting out of your own head, 162–69
getting perspective, 169–78
Gilbert, Daniel, 43–44, 163–64, 165
Gilovich, Tom, 7–9, 29–31
Goffman, Erving, 76
Grace, 104–5, 111
Grant, Heidi, 53
gratitude, expressing, xi–xii, xiii
"gratitude letters," xiii
Grice, Paul, 42–43
Grinstein, Amir, 47
Gwinn, Jason, 186

hackers, 93–95
Hallock, Kevin, 71
Harper's Bazaar, 184
Hart, Einav, 113
"having someone's ear," 20–21
Hayley, 182–83, 185–86
Healy, Paul, 51
Higgins, Tory, 20
Hill, Katie, 137–44, 141
hiring, inappropriate/sensitive questions and, 112–17

"illusion of courage," 86–87
inappropriate questions, 112–17
inclination to agree, 42–46
inducers, 163–65
influence
    becoming aware of, 160–61, 183–86, 187
    dark side of underestimating, 123–24
    embracing, 98
    experiencing your influence on others, 161, 178–90, 188–89
    feeling your influence on others, 161, 169–78, 189
    obliviousness and, 157–58
    perceived, 125–55
    responsibility and, 128, 131–37, 151–55, 193
    seeing, feeling, and experiencing your, 157–90
    seeing your influence on others, 161, 162–69, 189
    underestimation of, 131–37, 151–55, 157–58
    unseen, 1–27

influence strategies, harnessing power of being in the audience, 21–22
"insinuation anxiety," 77
"invisibility cloak illusion," 4–6, 8–10

Jahren, Hope, 110, 138–39
Jiang, Jia, 179–80, 181, 183, 185, 189–90
Joel, Samantha, 105–9
Joffe-Walt, Chana, 149
Johnson, Earl, 130
Jones, Ned, 163–64, 165
Jordan, Alexander, 113

Kawakami, Kerry, 92
Kelley, David, 152
Kennedy, John F., 152
Krauss, Bob, 18
Kronrod, Ann, 47, 48
Krzyzewski, Mike, 129
Kumar, Amit, xi–xii
Kushner, Jared, 3

LaFrance, Marianne, 89–91
Langer, Ellen, 39
Laschever, Sara, 182
Latané, Bibb, 77, 134–35
Lauer, Matt, 103, 139
leadership positions, inappropriate requests and, 128, 129–31
Lewinsky, Monica, 140–41, 143
Libby, Lisa, 166
lies, white, 100–103
"liking gap," 35–37

The Liking Principle, 37–38
listening, getting perspective by, 169–78
Loewenstein, George, 86
Louis C. K., 103
LuPone, Patti, 15

Margot, 105
Martin, Ashley, 116
Mathios, Alan, 72
McDonnell, Mary-Hunter, 176
McKinney, L. L., 145
Meara, 182–83
Medvec, Vicky, 7–9
Mehra, Rebecca, 158–59
mentalization, 13–14
#MeToo movement, 103, 111, 124, 139, 145, 178
microaggressions, 150–51
Milbank, Dana, 4
Milgram, Stanley, 81–82, 83, 85–86
mimicking, 22–26
misinformation, 100–103, 119–21, 124. See also "bullshitting"
Mitnick, Kevin, 93–95
money, offering, 61–65
Moody's, 99–100
Moore, Don, 51
Morgenson, Gretchen, 100
Motorola, 93–95
MSNBC, 4

Nagarajah, Ramesh, 149
negatives, focus on, 185–86
Nevils, Brooke, 139

Newark, Daniel, 61–62, 68
New Yorker, 105
New York Times, 4, 100, 110, 130
Nkinski, Naomi Tweyo, 150
Noah, Trevor, 19–20
"non-Duchenne smiles," 90–91
Nordgren, Loran, 176

Obama, Barack, 152
obliviousness, 1–2, 149
O'Brien, Soledad, 145
Ohanian, Alexis, 152
Oliver, John, 140–41
Oluo, Ijeoma, 50
organizational misconduct, 124
others, listening to, 169–78
"outbreaks," of behavior, 23–24
overconfidence, 30
    dangers of, 51
overkill, 46–51

Painter, Nell, 147–48
Pennycook, Gordon, 120
people of color, listening to,
    149–51, 178
perceived influence, 125–55
perspective(s)
    first-person, 166
    getting vs. taking, 151,
        169–78
    taking other perspectives into
        account, 131–37
    third-party, 165–69
Petrocelli, John, 118–19
Plous, Scott, 51
"pluralistic ignorance," 79–80
"politeness," 76

power
    abuse of, 139–42
    choice and, 131–37
    definition of, 128
    freedom from fear of embar-
        rassment and, 134–35
    inappropriate requests and,
        128, 129–31
    misreading of deference and
        friendliness and, 142–43
    obliviousness and, 149–51,
        157–58
    opportunity and, 152–53
    perceived influence and,
        125–55
    as responsibility, 128, 131–37,
        151–55
    systemic, 144–51
    underestimation of, 151–55,
        157–58
presence
    influence of, 10, 11–14
    value of showing up, 26–27
"the press of the situation," 133
principles, confidence in, 89–93
prosociality, 133
#PublishingPaidMe movement,
    145

race, Rejection Therapy and,
    185
racial invisibility, 147–48
racism, 91–92, 124, 144–48
    racial hierarchies, 147–48
    systemic, 146–48
Rauer, Erika, 15
recalibrating, importance of, 52

rejection, fear of, 178–90, 186,
189–90
Rejection Therapy, 178–90
representation, importance of,
26–27
requests
anxiety about making, 61–68,
73–74
difficulties of saying "no" to,
75–98, 103, 123
fear of making, 73–74
fundraising, 57–60, 69–72
large, 65–72
making, 53–74, 96–98
pessimism about responses,
54–60, 61–68, 72, 73–74
small, 57–60
responders, 163–65
responsibility
"diffusion of responsibility,"
78–80, 82
influence and, 128, 131–37,
151–55, 193
power as, 128, 131–37, 151–55
"reverse spotlight effect," 8–10
Reyna, Valerie, 41
Rivera, Lauren, 112–13
Roghanizad, Mahdi, 83–84
Romney, Mitt, 17
Roy, Deb, 120
Ruttan, Rachel, 176

Sabini, John, 77, 82–83
Sah, Sunita, 76–77, 116
Sandstrom, Gillian, 35–36,
159–60
Sankes, Josh, 129–31, 130, 154

Sassenberg, Kai, 153
Savani, Krishna, 135
Savitsky, Ken, 7–9
"saying-is-believing effect,"
20–21
saying "no"
difficulties of, 75–98, 103,
105–12, 123, 151, 188
over email, 81–84
Scholl, Annika, 153
Seinfeld, Jerry, 16
self-perception theory, 97
sensitive questions, 112–17
sexual compliance, 105–9
sexual harassment, 103–11, 124,
129–31, 138–39. See also
advances
Shea, Catherine, 116
Shteynberg, Garriy, 13–14
Silverman, Arielle, 186
Smith, Pamela, 135
Smithsimon, Gregory, 147
social connection, 32–33
social engineers, 93–95
social media, 32–33, 47, 145
invisible audience on, 121–22
misinformation and, 120–21
Spinoza, Baruch, 43
"spotlight effect," 8–9
Steffel, Mary, 170
subordinates
choice and, 131–37
relationships with, 137–44,
175–76
Sullivan, Shannon, 148
systemic power, 144–51
systemic racism, 146–48

Team In Training study, 57–58, 60, 65–66, 68

Trump, Donald, 3, 4, 17, 19–21

underconfidence, 30–33, 32–33, 47
    trouble with, 51–52

Van Boven, Leaf, 86, 186
visibility, 3–6
visualization, 162–69
Vogel, Ken, 3, 4
Vosoughi, Soroush, 120

Washington Post, 3–4
Wathieu, Luc, 47
Weinstein, Harvey, 103, 104–5, 123, 139

Wenzel, Bob, 129
white lies, 100–103
whiteness, 147–48
white people
    oblivious to their impact, 149–51
    systemic racism and, 144–49
Willard, Ralph, 154
Wilson, Johannes, 91
Woods, Melody Joy, 145
Woodzicka, Julie, 89–91

Xu, Amy, 61–62

Yin, Yidan, 135

Zitek, Emily, 113